Project Management

A Practical Guide

Dermot Duff &
John Quilliam

Production credits
All design, artwork and liaison with printers has been undertaken by Neworld Associates, 9 Greenmount Avenue, Harold's Cross, Dublin 12, www.neworld.com

Publisher: Management Briefs, 30 The Palms, Clonskeagh, Dublin 14.

Table of Contents

Acknowledgements

"Learn from the past, live in the present, plan for the future."
This book could not have been written without the support and
assistance of many people, seen and unseen. Our families and
friends have been important, along with our colleagues in the Irish
Management Institute and Trinity School of Business, and a wide range
of organisations whose encouragement and practical advice has been
invaluable.

We particularly want to mention those who contributed to the book or
reviewed its contents, notably Pat McGrath and his colleagues in Project
Management, Dermot Barry-Walsh of MSD, Ray Murphy of Strategic
Consulting, Vaida Sasnauskiene, Philip Nolan and Tom McCarthy of
IMI and many others who quietly helped or encouraged.

A particular dedication is made to Sean and Mary Duff and to Kathy
Quilliam for their forbearance throughout.

Dermot Duff &
John Quilliam

November 2010

Foreword

Dermot and John have captured within this short book, the essentials of Project Management that should benefit all newcomers to Project Management.

It is a very welcome addition to our developing series of Human Resource, Organisation Behaviour and General Management Books.

All of the books in the series aim to capture the essentials for busy Managers; essential knowledge and skill presented in an accessible and easy-to-read style.

A list of books already published within the series appears on the inside of the back cover. Also, on one of the last pages of the book, you will find a list of forthcoming titles which can also be viewed at our website www.ManagementBriefs.com.

We welcome any contact from you the reader; it will only improve our products and our connection to our reader population.

Frank Scott-Lennon
Series Editor
Frank@ManagementBriefs.com

November 2010

1

Understanding Project Management

Chapter outline
Understanding Project Management

"Experience keeps a dear school, but a fool
  will learn in no other."

Benjamin Franklin

→ What is a Project?
→ The Project Life Cycle - The Four Phases
   of a Project
→ Phase 1: Getting Started - Concept,
   Initiation, Feasibility and Inception
→ Phase 2: Detailed Planning
→ Phase 3: Implementation, Monitoring,
   Control and Closure
→ Phase 4: Completion
→ Deciding the Type of Project and the
   Approach Required
→ Assessing Project Manager Authority
→ Assessing the Organisation's Project
   Capability
→ Achieving Project Success

This is a practical guidebook for anyone about to manage a significant project.

The book offers real-world perspectives on common project problems, and avoids academic approaches and jargon. It explains clearly how to plan for success, how to manage stakeholders, how to avoid unwelcome surprises and how to form a viable team. It reveals the hidden flaws that undermine so many projects, and suggests ways to avoid the surprising pitfalls in managing and leading projects. Research shows that more than half of all significant projects end in serious disappointment, delivering little of the expected outcome, or greatly exceeding the expected time. Roughly one-third of projects are strategic 'misfits' that should never have even been started.

However, even a basic use of project management will greatly increase the chances of success.

What is a Project?

A project is a concerted, planned effort to secure a pre-defined outcome within a set time and budget. It is a temporary endeavour with a distinct beginning, middle and end.

Frequently, it is accomplished by a team effort, with team members often unfamiliar with each other, requiring the project manager to be skilled in team-building.

Examples of projects include change initiatives, business development campaigns, office re-locations, business start-up, product development, marketing launches, recruitment drives, software development and strategic plans.

The Project Life Cycle - The Four Phases of a Project

Projects can be considered to have a 'life' of their own, from project concept to completion, as shown below:

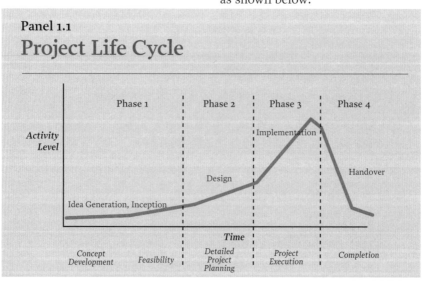

Panel 1.1
Project Life Cycle

A project can be regarded as having four distinct phases, from **initial idea** through detailed **planning** and **implementation** to **completion.**

Phase 1: Getting Started - Concept, Initiation, Feasibility and Inception

In this phase, the key activities are the generation of feasible approaches, the assessment of risk and reward, and the recognition of political difficulties with the project:

→ Finding and testing ideas

→ Recognising the key issues

→ Deciding the overall scale and scope of the project

→ Identifying the key risks and expected pitfalls

→ Setting indicative milestones

→ Proposing the project vision

→ Building early political support

→ Securing stakeholder commitment

→ Identifying critical assumptions and constraints

→ Setting up suitable project structures

Phase 2: Detailed Planning

This phase contains the classic project management planning activities, from the structuring of ideas into useful categories and on to the scheduling of resources:

→ Detailed resource and time plans

→ Getting the right people on board

→ Setting agreed schedules and deadlines

→ Deciding how to control the project

→ Ensuring project quality

→ Establishing how to manage the document trail

→ Generating and agreeing the baseline plan; 'Plan A'

→ Preparing contingencies; 'Plan B'

→ Setting the parameters that trigger the closure of any phase

→ Predicting the project's likely faults

→ Establishing a corrective action learning loop

Phase 3: Implementation, Monitoring, Control and Closure

In this phase, the activities move to implementation: monitoring if the tasks are on track and within budget, controlling deviations, and re-planning the project:

→ Discovering if the project is still on track

→ Recovering from project slippage

→ Dealing with difficult personality types

→ Predicting, avoiding and repairing political divisions

→ Maintaining morale and sustaining momentum

→ Problem-solving and dealing with unexpected issues

Monitoring if the tasks are on track and within budget, controlling deviations, and re-planning the project

Phase 4: Completion

In the completion phase, the emphasis is on getting the vital last tasks concluded and securing agreement from stakeholders that the job is completed, and that reward and recognition for a successful project is now due:

→ Securing final sign-off

→ Closing project accounts

→ Dealing with late issues

→ Getting recognition for accomplishments

→ Getting paid for work done

→ Assessing the project

→ Learning from the project

The overall project plan typically addresses the areas shown in the chart below:

Panel 1.2

Project Plan

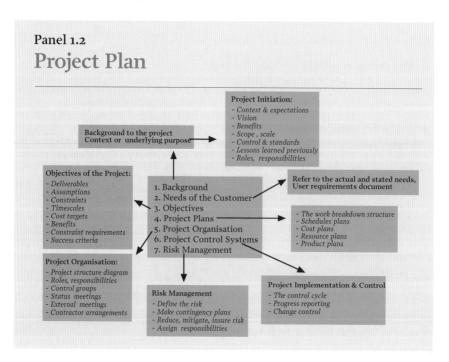

Project Initiation:
- Context & expectations
- Vision
- Benefits
- Scope , scale
- Control & standards
- Lessons learned previously
- Roles, responsibilities

Background to the project
Context or underlying purpose

Objectives of the Project:
- Deliverables
- Assumptions
- Constraints
- Timescales
- Cost targets
- Benefits
- Constraint requirements
- Success criteria

Refer to the actual and stated needs,
User requirements document

1. Background
2. Needs of the Customer
3. Objectives
4. Project Plans
5. Project Organisation
6. Project Control Systems
7. Risk Management

- The work breakdown structure
- Schedules plans
- Cost plans
- Resource plans
- Product plans

Project Organisation:
- Project structure diagram
- Roles, responsibilities
- Control groups
- Status meetings
- External meetings
- Contractor arrangements

Risk Management
- Define the risk
- Make contingency plans
- Reduce, mitigate, insure risk
- Assign responsibilities

Project Implementation & Control
- The control cycle
- Progress reporting
- Change control

Deciding the Type of Project and the Approach Required

Projects can be characterised by the degree to which methods have been established and by the concreteness of the outcomes. For example, construction projects have relatively clear specifications but change initiatives, on the other hand, they often have methods and outcomes that can only be described in vague terms. The figure below shows the four broad categories of project.

Project Types	
High Visibility	
Type 1: Classic projects	Type 2: Open-ended projects
Example: Construction Projects	*Example: Change Projects*
- Has clear methods and outcomes - Tasks & Role clearly defined - Emphasis is on project discipline - Detailed dependencies - Deadlines have clear sanctions	- Both methods & outcomes unclear - Needs strong sponsor - Disruption, ambiguity likely - Need to build relationships - Wide range of stakeholders
Type 4: Innovation projects	Type 3: Familiar projects
Example: Product development projects	*Example: Annual meeting*
- High uncertainty, major risks - Explore alternatives early - Focus on low-cost trials - Introduce or buy in innovations - Use simple planning	- Project resembles a known process - Stakeholders know their roles - Working relationship established - Estimates and schedules known - Low in political issues
Low Visibility	

A different style of project management is suited to each category of project:

Type 1: Classic projects - detailed planning, disciplined approach

Type 2: Open projects - flexible, diplomatic, political, leadership approach

Type 3: Familiar projects - require minimal project management tools

Type 4: Innovation projects require a light initial approach to generate ideas

The Classic (Type 1) approach to project management works best when the project has a clear specification, reliable estimates, a predictable sequence of events and a dedicated project sponsor; these conditions rarely exist, but under such circumstances, even very *complicated* projects (erecting industrial units, constructing bridges, scheduling advertising campaigns) can succeed. These require high degrees of co-ordination, discipline, strict planning and formal contractual relations.

Open-ended (Type 2) projects (such as change initiatives, product development, HR campaigns) are different; they are much less predictable, subject to human behaviour, organisational politics, unreliable peer support and uncertain rules of engagement. When project acceptance is uncertain, or when conflict is inherent, then a less prescriptive approach to project management is required, one that requires a tolerance for ambiguity, diplomacy and relationship building.

Familiar or routine (Type 3) projects, where the risks, roles and responsibilities are well known, are essentially processes, and therefore require only a lightweight or administrative style of project management.

A different approach again is needed to develop *Embryonic Innovation* (Type 4) projects, where ideas are not yet tested. In new business ventures, technological innovations or early-stage marketing trials, success is elusive. Good project management here depends initially on the ability to generate ideas, explore concepts and select winners rather than on a classic Type1 prescriptive approach.

Each of these project categories needs the appropriate approach and level of supervision; the project manager should be aware that no single style is universally applicable. Failure to adopt the right approach will lead to serious tension where project team members may feel micro-managed or neglected, the level of bureaucracy may be inappropriate or the pace may be unsuitable.

Assessing Project Manager Authority

The authority of a project manager depends in part on the centrality of projects in an organisation: for example, large car companies use 'heavyweight' project managers to drive the development of new models across different departments. These project managers have parity with senior executives such as division heads. In organisations without such a project focus, the project manager will have little direct power. He or she will often have to defer to others when seeking, for example, key people or special equipment; as illustrated below.

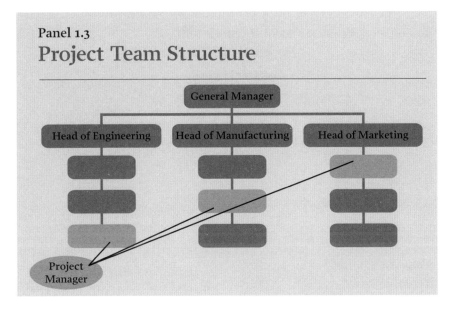

Panel 1.3

Project Team Structure

As can be seen in the above structure project managers can be drawn from a variety of levels. Project managers need to use the skills of influence to counter a lack of direct hierarchical power.

Assessing the Organisation's Project Capability

The project maturity 'staircase' illustrated below shows the evolution of project management maturity in an organisation, from basic competence to excellence. An organisation can benefit by systematically developing its project maturity through training, team development, benchmarking and continuous improvement.

The project manager will often have to defer to others when seeking, for example, key people on special equipment.

Panel 1.4

Project Management Maturity Levels

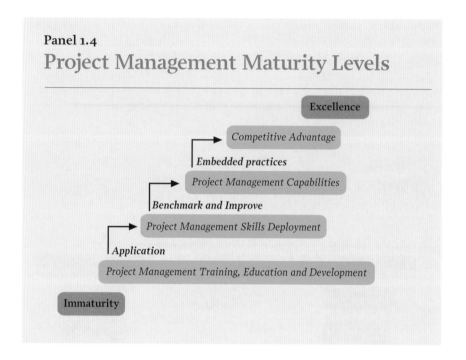

Panel 1.5

Project Management Maturity Levels

1. Common language - Basic knowledge of project management

2. Common process - Defined methods in widespread use

3. Singular approach - Project methods developed for particular situations

4. Project Process Improvement - Benchmarked & continually improved

5. Advanced Project Capability - Innovative - leading beyond industry norms

Achieving Project Success

In subsequent chapters, the core aspects of planning are described, including how to deal with influential stakeholders, manage risks and handle cost issues.

Panel 1.6

Tips for Project Success

→ Explore all options — refine the original idea by creating more potential solutions

→ Nail the brief — find out what is really required, and what is optional

→ Prioritise — when push comes to shove, know what

really matters in the project

→ Plan and re-plan until a viable plan emerges that satisfies all key criteria

→ Look ahead - the goal is to have no surprises, except pleasant ones

→ Cultivate stakeholders - sometimes it's not what you know, but who you know

→ Make deadlines count - if the first deadline is allowed slip, the rest will, too

→ Be ruthless with tasks but charming with people

→ Get power but use it sparingly - walk softly but carry a big stick

→ Communicate widely, then communicate again, then really communicate

→ Trust but verify - give people autonomy but have a system to check tasks

→ Build momentum: devise ways to get early successes, then keep that momentum

→ Learn early and often - watch for early signs of failure, and act on these

→ Break the project into discrete tasks - eat an elephant in small pieces!

The essence of project management is the fusion of intuition, common-sense and leadership with a systematic approach. Done correctly, projects provide huge satisfaction, career advancement, camaraderie - and hopefully some fun.

Summary of Chapter 1

→ Recognise the type of project involved, and adapt your management style to suit

→ Stay within the limits of the organisation's capability to deliver a project

→ Be prepared for shifts in priority as the project progresses through the lifecycle

→ Avoid the temptation to accept the project without sanity-checking its feasibility

→ Use your bargaining power from the outset to get the resources you need

→ Establish the limits of your authority — and your responsibility

→ Understand the different phases of a project

→ Be warned: the project may take longer and cost more than initially predicted!

2 Phase 1 - Getting Started

Chapter outline
Phase 1 - Getting Started

"The proper method for hastening the delay
  of error is by teaching each man to think for
  himself."

William Rodwin

→   Developing the Initial Brief
→   Developing the Project Concept
→   Phase 1 - Initial phase - Kick-off
    Meeting Agenda
→   Dealing with the Classic Triple
    Constraints
→   Handling the Initial Request to Manage
    the Project
→   Generating Potential Solutions
→   Performing a Feasibility Analysis

Developing the Initial Brief

This critical initial phase is often the most neglected phase of a project. This is perhaps because of its abstract nature, but it is at this conceptual stage that the seeds are sown for success - or failure.

The first step in defining the project is to develop an initial brief that explains the:

→ need to be satisfied

→ core purpose

→ expected scope and scale

→ known constraints

→ risks, and

→ agreed deliverables or outcomes expected.

The initial brief needs to be subjected to critical scrutiny, with an emphasis on exploring the costs, risks and efforts involved, compared to the expected benefits. A cost versus benefit analysis or a feasibility study is invariably a good investment, and should be undertaken even for 'obvious' projects. The business case needs to be developed and completed with projections, assumptions, risks and constraints.

Developing the Project Concept

The ultimate success or failure of the project is largely determined here in the initial phase. Attention must be given to developing the core concept, predicting risks, identifying stakeholders and selecting the core team.

The use of structured project start-up briefings or workshops is an excellent way to develop a fuller picture of the project.

Project launch workshops should agree a brief which covers the following:

→ Background and context: Needs, Wants, Options

→ Purpose, scope and high-level objectives

→ Key risks, constraints and assumptions

→ Preliminary budget

→ Overall timeline

→ Core team formation

→ Quality control and governance structures

Phase 1 is complete when all issues are satisfactorily resolved and when there is a definite collective responsibility felt both for the agreed outcomes and the process by which the project will deliver the intended value. The agenda below can drive Phase 1 activities.

Phase 1 - Initiating Phase - Kick-off Meeting Agenda

- → Introduction to the Project, Purpose, Vision
- → Personal introductions of team members and project organisation chart
- → Project scope and objectives
- → Key success factors in this initiative
- → Known risks, challenges and project constraints
- → Project approach: standards, methods and tools
- → Major roles and responsibilities
- → Key events, project timeline, major milestones
- → Quality assurance plan
- → Project management and schedule planning standards and guidelines
- → Centralised documentation storage facility: on-line and physical storage
- → Time collection and project status requirements
- → Training and induction schedules
- → Project expectations and next steps
- → Lessons learned from previous post-project reviews
- → Unresolved issues, assignments, including target completion dates

Dealing with the Classic Triple Constraints

A project is usually 'triple-constrained' by the contending criteria of quality, cost and time; a project should reach a defined goal, yet it shouldn't exceed the budgeted cost and it should also be completed on schedule. This triple constraint can be considered as a triangle of forces, with pressure potentially from all sides. A project that requires a total solution, in the shortest timeframe and at minimal cost, invariably produces extreme pressure. For example, a project to substantially increase market share in a few weeks with a minimal budget and few resources can easily become 'mission—impossible'.

15

The triangle shows a circle, indicating the location of the priority; here, it is in the cost corner. The circle can move depending on the project and its phase. It is important to establish the priority at an early stage so that decisions can be made more reliably.

If you are faced with the triple constraint, it will take an act of genius to reconcile the conflicting aspects. Try to agree which of the competing elements has priority; literally draw the project triangle and invite the sponsor to indicate which corner of the triangle is considered truly the most important.

For example, if a tight budget seriously reduces quality or extends the time scale, you can ask for verification that you are indeed expected to compromise project integrity or expected outcome for the sake of the budget.

This hopefully can lead to debate, as distinct to argument, about where any trade-offs can be made. If, on the other hand, the project sponsor will not debate project realities, you will at least be aware that the

project is destined for failure, and prepare accordingly.

The project triangle of triple constraints can be expanded in other dimensions, such as risk or scope, depending on the specific nature of the project. The degree of uniqueness or innovativeness required may be a critical dimension worth capturing in the diamond.

Handling the Initial Request to Manage the Project

Projects present the opportunity for individual progress and real achievement.

The effective project manager will be recognised and rewarded for the ability to achieve results, especially results through other people.

There is inevitably a strong temptation to acquiesce to a request from a more senior person to manage a project, even before the concept or risks are clarified but premature agreement, diving into action, and avoiding the hard issues are all temptations to be avoided. The project manager must stand back and recognise the key risks in the plan; a hasty, unstructured start usually brings a quick but disappointing finish.

Before agreeing to manage any project, draft an outline plan that addresses the main issues, and only proceed when sufficiently confident of success. Use the time prior to accepting the project to bargain for the resources and rewards you and the project need and deserve; this is one of the few occasions on which a project manager will have real power. Early identification of the crucial issues reduces the stress and effort in a project; the expert project manager confronts issues early, while inexperienced project managers may pay a heavy price later for their original acquiescence, as illustrated below:

Panel 2.1

Project Stress Graph

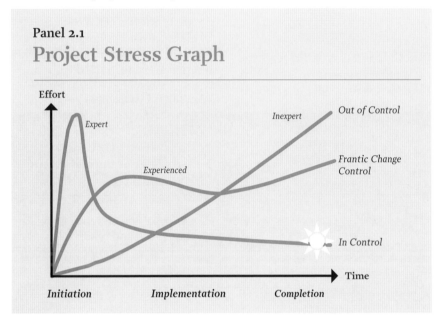

Generating Potential Solutions

Generating multiple solutions can help avoid reliance on a single project answer and produce innovative solutions by combining different options.

The solution matrix, shown below, helps brainstorm ideas and rank potential solutions. It promotes constructive debate and structures decision-making.

Assess the proposed approaches using criteria such as effectiveness, payback, or timeliness. Simple indicators such as Good, Fair, Poor work well but it can be worthwhile to award numerical scores - marks out of 10, for example.

Possible Solution	Effectiveness	Payback	Time	Total
A	6	4	7	17
B	4	5	7	16
C	7	3	4	14
D	2	8	5	15

17

Often, the initial idea is surpassed by subsequent suggestions; the real breakthrough is when proposed solutions are combined in entirely new ways.

Example: Tunnel Vision

When working abroad, my crew were faced with the problem of providing a river crossing for some indigenous people. The initial idea, from the native group, was for a kind of rough tunnel. This, however, would be ineffective, costly, time-consuming and uncertain.

Other suggestions, such as a bridge, were proposed and this led to a brainstorm of other ideas. Some, such as using a rope to cross the river, were initially regarded as simplistic, while others, like damming the river, were excluded because of the potential unintended consequences.

Solution	Effectiveness	Payback	Time	Total	Comment
Tunnel	1	1	1	1	Not viable
Bridge	8	2	2	32	Very expensive
Ferry Boat	5	3	5	75	Possibility
Raft	2	8	8	128	**Highest score**
Rope	1	10	10	100	Not useful alone
Dam	9	1	0	0	Too many unknowns

The final solution was a combination of some of the original proposals: ropes were used to lace together a series of rafts, so that the whole assembly became a floating bridge or pontoon, allowing the intended purpose (easy transit across the river) to be met.

The solution matrix can be made more accurate by systematically refining estimates of time and cost, perhaps even preparing comprehensive estimates and budgets; this allows objective and detailed comparison of options.

A valuable extension of the solution grid is to look for additional opportunities that can be exploited or provide synergy; kill two birds with the one stone by, for example, incorporating upgrades to a product in combination with changes made for regulatory purposes.

The above solutions address one-dimensional needs: other projects will need to address multiple needs and this invariably leads to a dilemma: a project might entail widespread consultation yet have a pressing need for speed. Such a dilemma requires creative thinking to resolve the contending needs.

Performing a Feasibility Analysis

For even the smallest projects, a feasibility study should be conducted as this will:

→ Give a clear understanding of the issues involved

→ Identify and evaluate many options, so that the best solution is found

→ Produce enough information so that options can be ranked

→ Result in a clear idea of the next steps

An initial feasibility study can help identify the benefits and disadvantages by listing 'pro' or 'con' aspects of the respective proposals:

Proposed Solution	Pro *(factors favouring)*	Con *(factors against)*
A	Satisfies client ego	Outside our expertise, slow
B	Simple, cheap, quick	Unstable, dangerous
C	Relatively easy, quick, costly	Hard to maintain

A good cost/benefit analysis is hampered by the difficulties in obtaining critical facts, maintaining objectivity, surfacing latent assumptions and assessing non-obvious risks. It is still an essential activity and it is aided by generating a number of solutions and analysis of the pros and cons.

Summary of Chapter 2

→ Look beyond the initial ideas by exploring alternative solutions

→ Brainstorm ideas and combine them to produce the optimum solution

→ Use the Project Management triple constraint triangle to agree the key priorities

→ Assess ideas through constructive debate; rank ideas according to the priorities

→ Invest in a feasibility study, however basic or short

→ Limit the project scale and scope to increase the project's chances of success

→ Generate potential solutions

→ Learn from the organisation's typical failure modes to identify key success factors

→ Ensure that there is a sense of collective responsibility for the project

3

Phase 2 - Developing the Project Plan

Chapter outline
Phase 2 -
Developing the Project Plan

"A man steers well who reaches the port for
 which he started."

Lucius Seneca, 4 BC — 65 AD

→ Phase 2 - Starting the Detailed Planning
    - Work Breakdown Structure
→ Work Breakdown Structure - Example
→ Estimating Task Duration and Effort
    Required
→ The Uncertainty of Estimates
→ Scheduling the Sequence of Tasks
→ Building the Activity Network Diagram
→ Identifying the Critical Path
    through the Project
→ Optimising the Schedule
→ Allocating Resources in the Plan
→ Identifying and Relieving the Project
    Bottlenecks

Crucial to project planning are the inter-related activities of estimating time, costs and other resources required and of scheduling tasks and events. These activities rely on logic but are also liable to human bias and game-playing. For example, it is often a question of judgement or opinion as to how long a task should take or who is best equipped to perform that task.

Phase 2 - Starting the Detailed Planning - Work Breakdown Structure

Having agreed the goals and the proposed solution in Phase 1, the actual planning process starts with a listing of the discrete tasks needed to achieve the agreed goal. This will be little more than an incomplete and unstructured 'to-do' list. To check for missing tasks, and to organise the tasks in a more structured format, a Work Breakdown Structure (WBS) can be used. A WBS is simply a hierarchical structuring of the tasks involved, organised in the format of an organisation chart, as shown below:

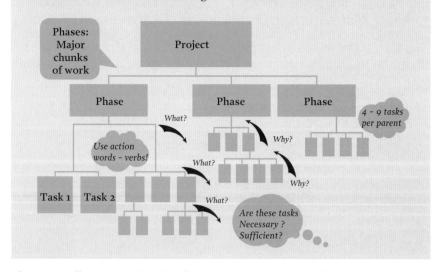

The WBS allows examination for omissions and overlap, and starts the process of sequencing the tasks in logical order. The WBS need not be exhaustively detailed, but should stop when a task can be considered to be performed by a suitably trained person.

Work Breakdown Structure - Example

For example, the construction of a sun-room extension onto the side of a house might have phases such as Planning, followed by actual Construction, then Installation, as shown on the next page:

Panel 3.1
Work Breakdown Structure

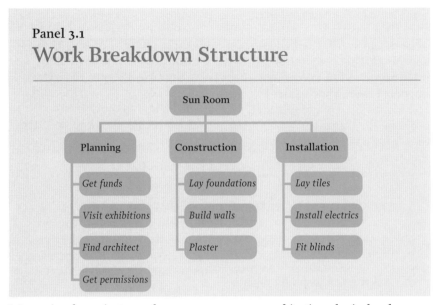

Many simple projects can be scheduled without a WBS but it is still good practice to create this structure, if only as a means to identify missing tasks.

The listing of tasks is then sequenced in time-logical order called a Gantt chart, as shown below. The length of the "bars" represents the duration of each task. The tasks are shown in groups, known as phases in the WBS.

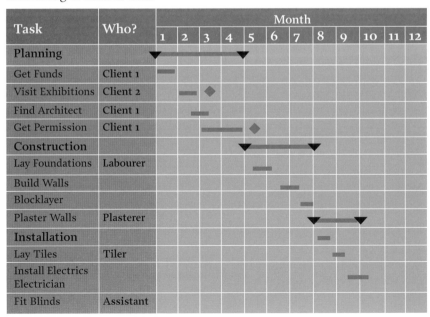

Task	Who?	Month											
		1	2	3	4	5	6	7	8	9	10	11	12
Planning		▼				▼							
Get Funds	Client 1	▬											
Visit Exhibitions	Client 2		▬	◆									
Find Architect	Client 1		▬										
Get Permission	Client 1				▬	◆							
Construction						▼		▼					
Lay Foundations	Labourer					▬							
Build Walls							▬						
Blocklayer								▬					
Plaster Walls	Plasterer								▼	▼			
Installation								▬					
Lay Tiles	Tiler								▬				
Install Electrics Electrician										▬			
Fit Blinds	Assistant												

23

The Gantt or Bar Chart above shows the assigned 'resource' or person, and shows the logical dependency between tasks; in other words, what tasks must finish before the subsequent task can begin. For complicated projects, the Gantt chart will need to be used in conjunction with the Activity Network Diagram, described later in this chapter.

Estimating Task Duration and Effort Required

Estimating the duration and effort of a task can be a simple exercise if the task is predictable and mechanistic. In such cases, previous records, industry norms, agreed rates or other standards can be reliably applied. Where the task depends heavily on human factors, the accuracy of any estimate falls sharply, and an extra 'allowance' needs to be made to cover the uncertainty of information.

This allowance is different to 'contingency', which is a specific reserve or alternative that may be called upon in the case of specific risks becoming actual.

The explorer Amundsen carried ten times more food and fuel per person than Scott, whose team died from starvation - "In a journey of four months, Scott had not allowed for four days of bad weather", it was noted. Amundsen, aware that Scott occasionally could not locate food placed in the Antarctic

wastes, put in place a control grid to guide him, setting out large flags to mark his food caches. He also put flags for five miles on either side, and each flag was numbered to guide the explorers to the food.

The Uncertainty of Estimates

A good plan is one that is sufficiently reliable that it can become the basis for effective decision-making. The further one has to forecast, the greater the degree of uncertainty.

The reality is that early forecasts have large uncertainties; the degree of uncertainty normally reduces as the project progresses and as more information becomes available.

Note that estimates often tend to be unduly optimistic, even if the estimator actually believes them to be pessimistic; remember that research indicates that projects invariably finish later and cost more than predicted.

Proper planning incorporates some flexibility or reserve in the schedule. So-called 'agile' plans recognise that many projects, particularly IT projects, contain so many unknown factors that traditional, linear planning is inadequate; instead, these 'agile' plans are based upon short, intense trials, and then updated in light of actual achievements.

24

Scheduling the Sequence of Tasks

Scheduling involves sequencing tasks in a preferred order; the actual order depends on the urgency of the project, the resources available and the tolerance for risk-taking.

Projects with many simultaneous activities (or with little allowance for uncertainty) are subject to higher risks to the schedule.

The critical path is the sequence of events in a project path, which if delayed, results in a consequent delay to the overall project timeline. 'Critical' in this case means time-critical; other events may be more 'critical' from a risk perspective.

Building the Activity Network Diagram

The 'activity network diagram' illustrates the sequence, timing and duration of tasks in the project. It can also be used to indicate which tasks are critical to complete on time so that the final project end date is not delayed. The activity network diagram is a key part of the Programme Evaluation & Review Technique (P E R T) used to great effect on the Polaris submarine project, and popular ever since.

The order of tasks is determined by the logic of the situation: building walls cannot start until the foundations are finished. This is a 'finish-to-start' relationship, diagrammatically shown as follows:

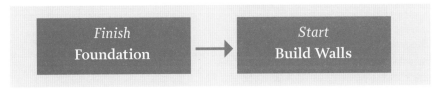

The above tasks are to be done 'in series', one following the other; some tasks can be done 'in parallel' with other tasks. For example, some earthmoving or landscaping could be laid once the foundations above are laid; this could be done in parallel with building walls, shortening the overall schedule but increasing complexity by performing two tasks simultaneously:

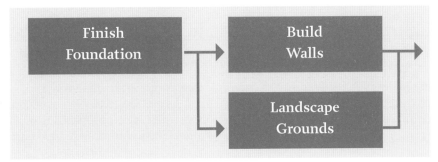

Shown below are the four forms of logical interdependency between related tasks:

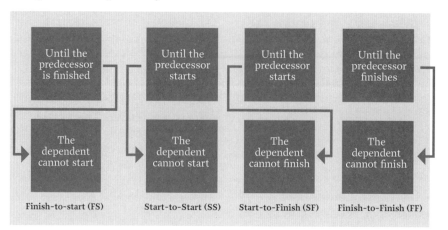

Until the predecessor is finished | The dependent cannot start — Finish-to-start (FS)

Until the predecessor starts | The dependent cannot start — Start-to-Start (SS)

Until the predecessor starts | The dependent cannot finish — Start-to-Finish (SF)

Until the predecessor finishes | The dependent cannot finish — Finish-to-Finish (FF)

The 'Finish-to-Start' (FS) dependency described earlier is the most prevalent, but a planner might need to depict a situation where a dependent task cannot start until the predecessor starts. An example of such a 'Start-to-Start' (SS) logic would be where planting shrubs cannot start until landscaping has started (it might be desirable but not essential to only start planting shrubs when all the landscaping is finished).

The third situation is where the dependent cannot finish until the predecessor starts; an example of such a 'Start-to-Finish' (SF) logical connection might be where a technician cannot finish an operation until a colleague has started other work.

Finally, there are situations where the finish of two tasks is interdependent; an example of a 'Finish-to-Finish' (FF) dependency might be, in the above example, the granting of certificates from the architect and the local authorities before the project can be finalised.

Note that the above tasks show duration (time elapsed); it is usual to also indicate how much 'effort' will be invested in those tasks during the elapsed time; a task, such as negotiating a mortgage on the construction, might need three weeks 'duration' but the 'effort' over that period might total only three days. This is generally represented as a percentage: in this case, the percentage is 20% (3 days spread over 3 weeks or 15 working days).

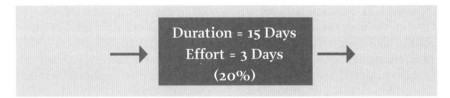

Duration = 15 Days
Effort = 3 Days
(20%)

Instead of allocating a particular person to a task, a type of resource can be indicated: in the example above, instead of specifying which painter will paint the walls, just the 'paint department' might be nominated, assuming interchangeable abilities. If resources are over-allocated, the effort will total over 100%, meaning that more additional resources are needed, or the task must be re-planned.

Panel 3.2

Supporting Tasks

Note that many plans lack many indirect or supporting tasks, such as meetings, communication sessions, decision-making efforts, report-writing, and milestone reviews. Other ignored areas include re-work, archiving, team-building activities and conflict management sessions; these can be lengthy and stressful activities. Add these tasks (perhaps with disguised titles!), along with some other 'buffers' so that the plan is actually realistic. Such overhead is effort that does not go to the core activities of the task but is still required - a sort of 'real world' cost of actually doing the work. Any omitted tasks are usually left to the unfortunate project manager!

Identifying the Critical Path through the Project

If every task in a project follows sequentially, then every task is on the critical path, as a delay on any task would delay the overall completion of the project. Most projects, however, have a number of tasks scheduled in parallel, and this presents the challenge of identifying which path through the network is 'critical'.

For example, if it is planned that, after constructing the exterior of a house, building the garden wall (which will take a duration of 5 days) will take place at the same time as decorating the interior (which will take a duration of 8 days), then the decorating task is on the critical path; it starts at the same time, but takes 8 days as opposed to 5 days, and therefore any delay there will delay the overall project end-date. The difference in duration between the two tasks is 3 days (8 days - 5 days); this is known as slack or float, meaning that a delay of up to 3 days duration in building the garden wall should not affect the overall project completion

date. If the wall builder asks for up to 3 days off, or if you assign him another task (of up to 3 days duration) then the overall project completion should not be adversely affected.

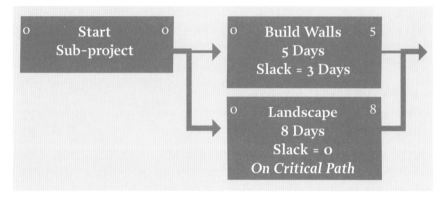

The tasks on the critical path are highlighted with **heavy lines** or with colour.

The start and finish times are shown on the left hand side and right hand side (respectively) of each task box. Where the project consists of a sequential series of tasks, only the top boxes (earliest start and earliest finish) are used.

In more complicated projects, where there are parallel paths, the bottom boxes are used to show latest start and latest finish times; this is needed to calculate project slack. The amount of slack is invariably shown, to help planning and prioritisation. Finally, an identification number for each task is usually shown:

Earliest Start	Task Identifier	Earliest Finish
	Duration	
Latest Start	Slack or Float	Latest Finish

In simple projects, the critical path and other calculations can be determined manually; in large or complicated projects, this is better done with specialised software.

28

Optimising the Schedule

Having made the initial draft plan, re-consider its suitability in practice; check for clashes with other projects, especially for critical resources (such as a key person busy on multiple projects). Re-plan if there are vital tasks at pressure periods (such as vacation periods or year-end rushes). Reconcile major events, such as milestone reviews, with planned vacations. Check for anomalies, such as an unreasonable schedule for the most crucial contributors, or Friday deadlines for most important tasks.

Remember not to schedule people to be 100% occupied; allow for training periods, illness, administrative activities — as a general rule, plan on 80% allocation, roughly 32 hours per standard working week.

Once the entire network of activities is drawn, this must be reconciled with the required date and budget; if these are not met, the network must be re-planned.

Panel 3.3

Major ways of reducing the overall timeline, and some constraints, are:

→ Re-negotiate the outcomes and methods involved, where feasible

→ Tighten the scope or defer certain features of the plan

→ Shorten the longest task as this provides the most potential for reduction

→ Perform more tasks simultaneously (in parallel)

→ Add extra resources to tasks on the critical path; use two block-layers not one

→ Two people performing a task require more effort than one person doing that task

→ Remember Brookes' Law: some tasks simply cannot be portioned out

→ Work weekends or overtime: this adds expense and increases burn-out risk

→ Incentivise an early project finish, with cash, rewards or concessions

→ Place sanctions, such as fines or loss of privileges, on lateness

→ Sub-contract any suitable, well-defined tasks

→ Use a finer timeline: sharpen the planning pencil.

Allocating Resources in the Plan

Resources, in project terms, are people, equipment, facilities and other assets that need to be deployed to achieve a task. For example, the installation of a computer network may require a technician with certain levels of experience or qualification; deploying multiple technicians may achieve an almost corresponding reduction in the time duration involved (but not the effort required, of course). This human resource can be a named individual or can be simply identified by organisation or by department (e.g. IT department). Agree who will actually perform the tasks, and what other resources are required.

Other resources frequently assigned include meeting rooms, as well as more obvious resources such as machinery or plant. It is not usual to assign enabling equipment, such as phones or standard office equipment.

The amount and type of resources is frequently limited or may be constrained by other considerations (such as the number of technicians who can work simultaneously in a small space). Similarly, resources may be made available in minimum blocks of time; for example, technicians may be paid for a minimum of a day, even if they only work a few hours, and consequently, the project planner attempts to balance the work load to suit circumstances.

Identifying and Relieving the Project Bottlenecks

The capacity of a project is constrained by the capacity of the scarcest resource, termed the 'bottleneck'. The outflow from a bottle, for example, is constrained by the diameter of the neck. In a motorway system, the bottleneck could be the toll station. In a project, it is frequently the capacity of a particular machine or a specialist such as an IT expert.

Panel 3.4

Manage the bottleneck, not the entire system - Case

Well before a motorway reaches theoretical capacity, no traffic moves; throughput only improves when you add capacity and relieve the pressure on the bottleneck. The key is to find the bottleneck, exploit or relieve it and then find the ensuing bottleneck.

A manufacturer was in trouble: its new product was seriously delayed and over budget. A review highlighted that there were 60 different modules being designed but these were bottlenecked in the system; little was emerging from the product 'pipeline'.

Morale was low and a plan was desperately needed; while each module had a rough timetable, there was no master plan to cover the full product portfolio. Moreover, no single person was truly in charge and each department was competing for priority.

It emerged that all modules had to pass through a critical layout design activity, resourced by just one engineer – this was the bottleneck. It quickly became clear that the key was to schedule this work better and to immediately add capacity of any kind to relieve this bottleneck. The meticulous work involved meant that engineers were unwilling to do this more 'menial' work; instead, a capable technician was promoted to the role. His challenge would be to learn how to process the simpler modules within weeks, thereby allowing the experienced technician to concentrate on the more intricate work.

The schedule was organised so that any module that could be quickly finalised was pushed to the top of the queue, and all efforts were devoted to getting the module finalised – not delayed due to minor details. Within weeks, output soared and the lost schedule was recovered. Morale improved, and there was new belief in planning.

Summary of Chapter 3

→ Check for project completeness – include invisible tasks like communicating ideas

→ Make your estimates realistic by allowing extra time and resources for novel tasks

→ Allow extra time and resources for long-term tasks; uncertainty increases with time

→ Schedule tasks in sequence rather than in parallel, where possible, to reduce risk

→ Allow buffers between tasks so that delays are not relayed throughout the project

→ Know which tasks on the project pathway are critical; focus on these critical few

→ Remember: Those who must do the work must plan the work

→ Manage the bottleneck, as it is the limiting factor in the project

→ Deliberately make a plan that is contingent on certain events transpiring.

4

Managing Risk

Chapter outline
Managing Risk

"A risk is an unwelcome event that might happen: an issue is a risk that has already happened."

Project maxim

→   Risk Management Steps
→   Types of Risk
→   Risk Impact / Probability Matrix
→   Managing Risk, Opportunity and Value
→   Classic Flaws in Organisations
→   Blindness to Habitual Risk

The purpose of risk management is to identify threats to project success and to eliminate, mitigate or offset their impact. Analysis of the risks may also identify opportunities that should be pursued to provide additional benefit to the project or the organisation as a whole.

Risk management is a deliberate and systematic process, with the following main steps.

Risk Management Steps

❶ Identify the potential risks, using team members or, if needed, specialist advisors:

→ Assess each risk and assign a probability based on available evidence

→ Assess and prioritise each risk in terms of severity or consequences

→ Develop a risk strategy for selected risks.

Types of Risk

There are different types of risk, including self-induced risks such as deficiencies in project management itself; Listed below are the principal types of risk that face the project manager.

Panel 4.1
Types of Risk

Risks can be categorised in several ways:

Project Risk - the threats to the management of the project, such as absence of key personnel or scarce resources, that can seriously impact project outcomes

Business Risk - the economic or strategic threats arising to the organisation should project outcomes not be realised

Technical or Operational Risks - Risk from failures in service delivery, from technical breakdowns or system outages

Reputational and Political Risks - threats to brand or organisational goodwill, or impact of politically disaffected or actively hostile stakeholders

Natural Risks - threats to the project from unfavourable conditions or natural disasters

For each risk, there are typically four approaches:

❶ Mitigate the effect and/or reduce the impact

❷ Reduce the likelihood of the risk, by taking preventative measures

❸ Offset the risk, by buying insurance or by out-sourcing the task

❹ Accept the risk without modification

To decide which approach to use, analyse the risk with regard to its likelihood and consequence. The matrix below shows risk likelihood on a spectrum from 'Rare' to 'Almost Certain'; similarly, it shows risk consequence from 'Severe' (such as loss of life or complete operational failure) to 'Insignificant'. It is the combination of likelihood and consequence that determine overall risk profile.

Panel 4.2
Risk Impact / Probability Matrix

Impact	Risk almost certain	More than likely	Likely	Unlikely	Rare
Severe	Extreme	Extreme	Extreme	High	Medium
Major	Extreme	High	High	Medium	Medium
Medium	High	High	Medium	Medium	Low
Minor	High	Medium	Low	Low	Insignificant
Trivial	Medium	Low	Low	Insignificant	Insignificant

Extreme	*Manage as emergency*
High	*Manage proactively*
Medium	*Manage strategically*
Low	*Manage systematically*
Insignificant	*Accept or Ignore*

Each risk can then be assessed to deicide 'counter-measures' that mitigate the effect or reduce the probability. Some risks may simply be 'accepted' as risks worth taking but others may need to be off-set through out-sourcing or by insuring the risk.

The table below is a template for identifying the specific risks, their probabilities and impacts, together with counter measures and risk strategy.

It is useful to also assign a risk 'owner' to manage the risk and initiate a planned response.

Managing Risk, Opportunity and Value

Specific Risk	Identify potential risks
	→ Technical
	→ Political
	→ Business
	→ Natural
Probability	Decide probability over relevant timeframe
	→ High
	→ Medium
	→ Low
	→ Severe
Impact	Assess impact
	→ Severe
	→ Major
	→ Minor
	→ Insignificant
Counter-measures	Agree specific solutions, remedies or mitigations
Strategy	Decide whether to
	→ Avoid risk
	→ Reduce impact
	→ Reduce probability
	→ Transfer risk
	→ Accept risk as is
Response Owner	Decide who will monitor each risk and lead the response

Every project contains risk, but not all elements of a project produce equal value. The successful project manager identifies those parts of a project that deliver real value at acceptable risk.

The good project manager combines the two aspects in a risk/value strategy, as shown in the figure below, where the top right quadrant has valuable but risky elements, and the bottom left quadrant has low-risk, low-value elements. Note that the top left quadrant shows elements that are risky but low value, and the bottom right quadrant has valuable elements with relatively low risk — 'the juicy bits'.

High Risk	Quadrant 1 *AVOID* High Risk Low Value	Quadrant 2 *DO FIRST* High Risk High Value
Low Risk	Quadrant 3 *DO LAST* Low Risk Low Value	Quadrant 4 *DO SECOND* Low Risk High Value
	Low Value	**High Value**

Because they are the highest value, and expose the risks earliest, Quadrant 2 items should be attempted first. The true viability of the project will therefore become clearer, while high value is added.

Similarly, *Quadrant 4* items produce value but at low risk and should be attempted next.

If possible, the low-value, high-risk *Quadrant 1* items should be avoided (as they are not worth the risk).

The low-risk and low-value *Quadrant 3* items should be left until last.

Ignoring risk is foolhardy, but equally treating all elements as having equal value is naïve; a better strategy is to address both risk and value simultaneously, as shown above.

Classic Flaws in Organisations

Just as people have characteristic strengths and weaknesses, so do organisations; if recent projects have been undermined by a recurring cause (such as a dysfunctional structure, poor culture, and/or divisive politics) then that genetic flaw is likely to impact your project also. Some of these flaws can be managed, but at

> Just as people have characteristic strengths and weaknesses, so do organisations.

the expense of extra overhead or lower efficiencies.

For example, a not-for-profit organisation prided itself on the autonomy of its specialist staff; when projects called for their collaboration, co-operation was so alien to them that it was impossible to succeed without adding facilitators, increasing efforts at consensus formation and other means of conscious team building.

As another example, a multinational company had such a labyrinthine structure that it was difficult to know with any certainty who really had power. The solution was to devote extra effort to clarifying roles and responsibilities, and to devising escalation strategies in the event that decisions would get bogged down in the organisational matrix.

Blindness to Habitual Risk

When two risks occur simultaneously, calamity can occur. Each risk, though small and unlikely, when compounded can have a disastrous effect on a project. The Challenger space rocket catastrophe happened because defects in the o-rings on the Challenger space rocket were worsened by unusually low temperatures at the Florida launch centre.

Curiously, the defects had not proven a problem previously and this served to obscure the danger in freezing conditions. Successive pleas by concerned engineers went unheeded, with management rationalising the risks. In desperation the engineers submitted hand-written documents to highlight the issues,

37

but NASA interpreted this as sloppiness, not desperation, and proceeded regardless.

Later, astronaut Mike Mullane, who flew three Apollo missions, would describe how crews became inured to even potentially fatal risks after the risks didn't materialise initially; he termed this risk blindness as 'the normalisation of deviance'. He explains how the Challenger blew up on its second mission, with complete loss of life, partly as a result of NASA personnel gradually becoming blind to risks that were originally considered lethal.

Panel 4.3
Three Mile Island and 'Normal' Accidents

Industrial accidents often happen from a chain of minor events. For example, the Three Mile Island nuclear station almost melted down in 1979, because of a series of small, 'routine' defects. The plant's water filter blocked, inadvertently tripping two valves and stopping the flow of cold water into the plant's steam generator. As 'bad luck' would have it, someone had closed the valves in the back-up system. Worse, a repair tag obscured that particular indicator in the control room. The next level of back-up valve wasn't working either. Not only that, but the gauge for that valve also gave a false indication. Five separate faults conspired to bring the nuclear reactor close to melt-down. The moral of the story: run a tight ship and keep the decks clear.

Remember that no project is risk-free; plan with pessimism but then execute with optimism, keeping alert to the dangers and having responses ready. You wouldn't drive a car without a spare wheel, but neither would you take four spares. Seat belts may be a nuisance but are to be insisted on. *Be careful in planning but bold in execution.*

Remember that no project is risk-free; plan with pessimism but then execute with optimism, keeping alert to the dangers and having responses ready.

Summary of Chapter 4

→ Good project management avoids surprises; consciously prepare a risk strategy

→ All risks can be quantified, with sufficient research

→ Identify specific risks, decide counter-measures and assign risk 'owners'

→ Link risk with value; complete a risk/value matrix

→ Realise which risks are probable and significant and prepare accordingly

→ Prevention is better than cure; preparation reduces risks

→ Small risks accumulate; avoid disaster by generating risk awareness

→ Have an early warning system; use your team to forewarn of risks

→ Plan for any significant eventuality but then proceed with due confidence

"Risk comes from not knowing what you're doing."

Warren Buffett

5

Phase 3 -
Implementing
the Plan

Chapter outline
Phase 3 - Implementing the Plan

"Culture eats strategy for breakfast."
- Larry Bossidy

→ Use the Agreed Baseline to Monitor and Control the Project
→ Monitoring the Project Plan
→ Project Control
→ Change Control and Management
→ Common Human Factors in Planning and Execution
→ Student Syndrome and the use of Time Buffers
→ Use Deadlines and 'Birthlines' to drive behaviour
→ Plan Tasks as Discrete, Deliverable Blocks of Work with Observable Outcomes

Use the Agreed Baseline to Monitor and Control the Project

The plan should contain means of monitoring progress and of controlling the project through corrective action if slippage or deficiencies occur. This implies a need to have feedback on progress and a means of rectifying deviations from the 'baseline' plan.

The *baseline* is the version of the schedule that has been approved. When the deadline of the revised schedule is later than that of the baseline, the project has *slipped*.

Variance is the difference between the estimated effort in the baseline and the actual effort expended by the team.

Monitoring the Project Plan

Monitoring is facilitated by deliberately planning tasks in discrete units with verifiable deliverables and by having regular 'milestones' to mark the completion of phases or activities; for example, if planning a marketing campaign, schedule tasks such as the production of raw copy, preparation of first draft, editing of final draft, verification of legal aspects, confirmation of basic data, followed by specific milestones, each with pre-defined review criteria. This converts amorphous or lengthy tasks into manageable units of work with specific outcomes planned.

Avoiding Slippage

There is truth in the axiom that projects *'become years late a day at a time'.* Consequently it is vital to ensure that the initial milestones, including project start, are met.

Slippage in the early phases is a definite predictor of project runaway and every effort must be made to deliver initial tasks on time, even if this involves extra effort and pressure. As the project manager for the original IBM 360 mainframe, S.F.P. Brookes, said *"Deadlines must be concrete, specific, measurable events, defined with knife-edge sharpness".*

The micro-culture of any project is heavily influenced by these early efforts. The mantra is to remain *gracious with people but tough on tasks,* seeking ways to recover lost time, perhaps by providing additional resources.

Better yet, find more clever ways to achieve the same result. In any case, review the causes of impending failure, and consider whether the working assumptions were false or if the basis of estimation is flawed or if there are team or motivation problems.

Repeated instances signal deep problems in the project, such as poor selection of key personnel, motivational issues or planning that is simply unrealistic.

To develop better commitment, the plan should be evolved and planned by those who will perform the tasks. Except in certain situations (such as regulated projects) it is only in this way that real commitment and agreement can be achieved.

Project Control

Effective control systems have means by which emerging issues are signalled clearly as early as possible; think, for example, of fuel gauges in cars or of audible signals in the case of car lights being left on. Similarly, detectors and signals need to be built into projects to control unacceptable deviations from the plan, in time, quality, cost or other parameters.

Panel 5.1

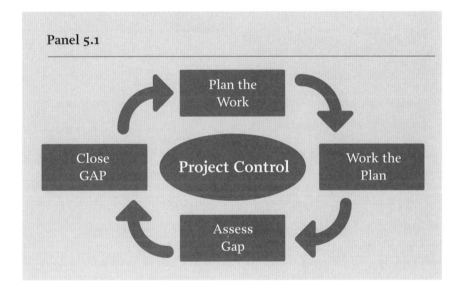

Partitioning of tasks into discrete work packages with defined and observable outcomes greatly assists project direction and control. Coupled with regular project updating and milestone reviews, this provides a means of planning and assessing progress.

If those who must execute the plan should be central to estimating and scheduling the associated tasks, then equally the status update should be similarly structured; ensure the task owners accept responsibility for progress reporting, and especially its veracity and accuracy.

Use simple self-managed systems, such as NASA's 'traffic lights' below, to highlight status, to note emerging risks and respond to red-alert warnings.

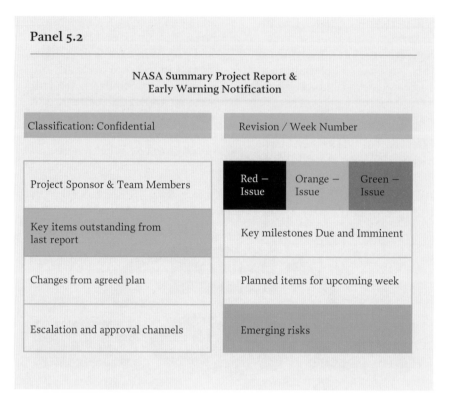

Panel 5.2

NASA Summary Project Report & Early Warning Notification

Classification: Confidential	Revision / Week Number

	Red – Issue	Orange – Issue	Green – Issue
Project Sponsor & Team Members			
Key items outstanding from last report	Key milestones Due and Imminent		
Changes from agreed plan	Planned items for upcoming week		
Escalation and approval channels	Emerging risks		

Project monitoring, control and rectification can be made habitual by encouraging such discipline from the outset of the project. The expert project manager confronts the issues, whether unrealistic goals, absence of critical resources or undue political pressure. It is essential to stand back and make the time to properly plan the project. If the key issues are not confronted, the project drifts, possibly ending in crisis.

The project manager must ensure an effective control system is in place and that there are resources to implement it. She must ensure appropriate review meetings take place, and that there is structured contact between stakeholders at appropriate levels. Change control is vital and a systematic process must be introduced that is communicated to everyone concerned.

"It is better to light a candle that curse the darkness"

Eleanor Roosevelt

Change Management and Control

The experienced project manager will concentrate on minimising the number of enforced changes. However, project changes are a fact of life; allowing scope creep is sure to lead to an accumulation of issues, but rejecting all change may lead to unsatisfactory project outcomes and may provoke resentment among clients and stakeholders. Review relevant requests, accepting only the necessary changes, and re-plan on this basis.

Change requests can even be turned to advantage, as ironically they give the opportunity to re-cast the project and perhaps benefit from a fresh approach.

Change control is a formal process used to ensure that a product, service or process is only modified in line with the identified necessary change. It is a fundamental process in quality control. It is formally used where the impact of a change could bring about severe risk on time, cost or quality of the end results.

Where information is received that may change the cost, scope, quality and/or time, the project manager should categorise that reason, and arrange an impact assessment.

This phase is where the quality of the planning and commitment becomes manifest; the successful project manager avoids surprises and reacts sensibly when issues arise.

Common Human Factors in Planning and Execution

To understand why projects fail so frequently, it is useful to consider some of the human factors that undermine decision-making.

For example, **Parkinson's Law** states that work expands to fill the time available, and the implication of this is that no task can ever be completed early.

Curiously, if a task were to finish early, it might not be in the achiever's interest to report this, as the 'reward' would be another task, and little thanks. In fact, it has been known that an early finish attracts the accusation that the estimation must have been poor, rather than the execution superb!

Furthermore, a project might not be in a position, because of planning rigidities, to take advantage of any early finish that does arise.

Additionally, the *Peter Principle* should be noted, for its effects on decision-making:

"In every hierarchy, people rise to the level of their incompetence"

Student Syndrome and the use of Time Buffers

Student syndrome is where the lifting of a deadline reduces pressure but induces slackness. For example, if a student under pressure to meet a deadline gets permission to submit a thesis later than originally expected, the student will invariably waste the grace period, only to find that the pressure returns towards the end of the extra period granted.

This is compounded by the inevitability that seemingly minor tasks (compiling the bibliography, getting the thesis bound) are invariably more onerous than anticipated.

Schedules are invariably padded, often significantly, to allow extra time for completion; the irony is that student syndrome undermines the felt sense of urgency, meaning that even artificially extended schedules fall victim to student syndrome.

The conclusion is that most projects are destined to inevitably finish late!

This can be offset by focusing on achieving early starts, meeting interim deadlines and packaging work into discrete packets. Add buffers that are not attached to specific tasks but are reserved as a block at the end of a group of tasks or a phase. This preserves the integrity of the overall plan while maintaining project discipline.

Even artificially extended schedules fall victim to student syndrome.

Use Deadlines and Birthlines to Drive Behaviour

To focus on starting on time, include a 'birthline' as well as a 'deadline'; after all, the power of an immutable deadline (such as a fixed event date) is clear. This also applies to the start, not just the finish, of an activity. Agree the start date, and monitor it closely: be sure to be vigilant that needed resources are actually in place and ensure a prompt start is made, with a fully understood brief and a committed team.

Plan Tasks as Discrete, Deliverable Blocks of Work with Observable Outcomes

Staying open to feedback will improve communication and help the project manager avoid schedule shocks. Parcelling tasks into small discrete chunks with defined outputs and observable deliverables helps clarify if a task is done or not. This also helps avoid the '90% syndrome'. This is where, for example, a software developer claims that 90% of the work is done, but in practice the difficult elements remain.

Summary of Chapter 5

→ Recognise delays and problems before they happen by designing a control system

→ Avoid scope creep and project drift by maintaining task discipline

→ Use 'traffic lights' to highlight significant emerging issues

→ Confront procrastination by insisting on the prompt starting of tasks

→ Keep the channels of communication open; use a variety of channels

→ MBWA: Manage By Wandering Around and showing interest

→ Understand human behaviour and avoid the typical syndromes

→ Formally batch and plan project changes

6

Building an Effective Project Team

Chapter outline
Building an Effective Project Team

→ Introduction to Team Building
→ Making Teams Effective -
   The Fundamentals
→ Team Development -
   How to form an Effective Project Team
→ Stages in Team Development
→ Dealing with changes over the course of
   the Project
→ Developing the Mission Statement
→ Team Guidelines
→ Sustaining Commitment over the life of
   the Project

Introduction to Team Building

Imagine you have just been asked by your boss to manage an important project, in an area of particular interest to you. You have been suggesting for some time that such a project should be initiated, so you are delighted to be given the responsibility for seeing it through. The boss has assigned a number of people from different areas of the business to form the project team that will work with you.

This will be your first opportunity to lead a project, and as you begin to think through the implications of your new role, naturally you pay a lot of attention to the task you have to undertake, and consider technical, logistical, and operational aspects.

You will also recognise that there is another aspect of the project that will need attention - the people that will form your team.

→ How well do you know them?

→ Do they know each other?

→ Have they worked together before?

→ How well do they understand the project?

→ How committed are they to its aims?

→ How will they get along with each other?

→ Will you be able to work with them?

Your ability to successfully deliver the project will in large measure depend on your ability to get high performance from this group of people.

The project manager must balance three interlinked requirements:

Task - getting the job done and delivering the project outcome,

Individual - motivating the individual members to perform to their potential, and

Team - maintaining the commitment and cohesion of the unit.

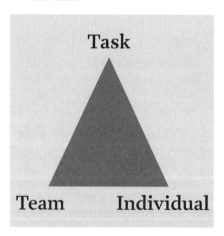

This is a useful way of thinking about the job of project management. The Task is in the pre-eminent position in the model, and this is as it should be. Delivering on the project objective is clearly the primary aim of the manager, and that's where the main emphasis of this book lies, but the others (Team and Individual) support and overlap with the task, meaning that successful outcomes depend on integration of all three.

Panel 6.1

What exactly is a Team?

Simple, it's a group of people committed to a common objective; but that could equally apply to a bus queue!

There are other factors needed if we are to have a real team:

→ People bring complementary skills to the team

→ They are committed to a common approach and performance goals

→ They share a sense of accountability for the success of the project

→ The team is limited in size: this may vary depending on the nature of the task, but 25 is probably the upper limit for one manager. As a rule of thumb, the manager should be able to make eye contact with all team members during meetings. It's no coincidence that sports teams typically have less than 18 members.

Making Teams Effective — The Fundamentals

➊ Pay attention to Process

Process refers to how we do things, as opposed to Content, or what we do.

Content issues are of course vital to success. They include:

→ Setting objectives

→ Gathering information

→ Deciding what has to be done

→ Action planning

→ Carrying out the work

→ Checking progress

→ Comparing results with objectives

Project managers have to be equally aware of the Process issues, such as:

→ Who will take the leadership role?

→ How will we plan & control our time?

→ How will we make decisions?

→ How will we make sure everybody contributes their ideas?

→ How will we keep track of decisions made?

These are critical issues whenever people come together to work in a team, irrespective of the team's task.

② Communicate

Talking, listening, sharing information, co-ordinating, disagreeing - all the elements in the continuous interaction of people — are a key element of team effectiveness. Project managers need to be sensitive to the mood and tone of communication as a basis for interpreting what is going on in the team. They also need to realise that communication is an *on-going* activity and that they should regularly question themselves as to whether or not they are providing all of the information that the team requires in a timely manner.

③ Build and Maintain Team Cohesion

Team members' behaviour can be classified as Task based or Maintenance. Task behaviours help the group do its work, and include:

→ Organising

→ Co-ordinating

→ Planning

→ Initiating

→ Seeking or providing information

Maintenance behaviour is focused on strengthening team cohesion, team spirit and morale, and includes:

→ Supporting

→ Encouraging

→ Reducing tension

→ Paying attention to team member's feelings

Effective teams are characterised by members who share a sense of accountability for success which they demonstrate through task & maintenance behaviours.

④ Norms

These are the rules, assumptions and traditions that govern behaviour in the team. Because project teams typically have a relatively short life and are composed of a disparate group with loyalties to other teams and groups in the organisation, the project manager needs to pay particular attention to ensure that appropriate norms of performance and behaviour are set and agreed.

⑤ Problem Solving and Decision Making

The ability to solve problems and make decisions is an essential element of an effective team. Participation by all in problem solving and decision making is desirable. However, it is not always feasible, and sometimes the manager has to exercise formal authority. The important point is that, whatever the method of problem solving and decision making employed by the team, it should be clearly communicated, understood and accepted by all as appropriate in the circumstances of the project.

❻ Leadership

Leaders of teams need to be aware of Process as well as Task issues. An over emphasis on the formal authority of the leader can risk inhibiting the growth of the team and the sense of shared responsibility. Leaders need to be flexible in their approach so as to accomplish the task and maintain the cohesion of the team.

Team Development – How to form an Effective Project Team

When you meet your team for the first time, there are some questions you must consider. Have the team members been assigned to the team on a part time basis? If so, they will be aware of potential conflicts between their regular task and their role on the team, and their instinct will almost certainly be to prioritise the needs of their 'day job' and the requirements of their line manager. So, as project manager you must expect, at best, divided loyalty, and consequently a challenge to motivate them to a high level of commitment to the project.

Newly assigned team members may not readily see how they can contribute to the project or may not be accustomed to communicating with colleagues

from different departments or disciplines; they may not be skilled in dealing with the tensions that can arise in situations of role ambiguity or interpersonal conflict.

Basic Concerns

How can the project manager address these challenges to build a cohesive team?

A good starting point in discussing these issues is to understand the 'basic concerns' that are likely to influence any new team members.

Psychologists have identified some basic concerns that people involved in any social interaction will experience:

→ **Acceptance concerns:**
  - Formation of trust
  - Acceptance of self and others
  - Anxiety and how to decrease it
  - Confidence and how to increase it

→ **Data/Issues/Norms Concerns:**
  - How we should communicate feelings, perceptions, ideas
  - Social norms and how they should be expressed

→ **Goal Formation Concerns:**
  - How our goals are set
  - How we solve problems
  - How we make decisions

→ **Control/Structure Concerns:**

- Regulation
- Co-ordination

Members of a project team will be no different, and in the early stages of a project a manager should expect that the members of the team will be dealing with some or all of these concerns. It should also be noted that Goal Formation and Control/Structure represent a comfort zone for managers — there can be a tendency to focus on these aspects in their initial meetings with the team.

It would however be a mistake to ignore the Acceptance and Data concerns, because if they are not acknowledged and addressed early on they can undermine the cohesion of the project team.

Panel 6.2
Stages in Team Development

Recognition of the need to address these human concerns is at the heart of the idea that teams need to go through a series of stages before they become fully effective. The stages are:

❶ The **Tentative** stage, when the Acceptance concerns are likely to be high. Individual team members are likely to be polite, anxious to please and keen to get started on

activities, but watchful, guarded and impersonal.

❷ The **Assertive** stage, where team members get over their initial tentativeness and begin to challenge, question and confront. Concerns about Data, Structure and Control come to the fore, and energy and anger can emerge as individuals push for position and seniority.

It is important that managers realise that this is normal and to be expected, and if managed effectively will lead to the next stage.

❸ The **Normative** stage represents a level of maturity as relationships are solidified, work practices agreed, and a sense of team spirit emerges as people get greater clarity about their objectives and how they can attain them. Commitment, trust and openness grow, and the team is positioned for the final stage.

❹ The **Productive** stage, when there is an emphasis on performance and an expectation of success. The challenge for the project manager is to maintain this momentum of high performance over the duration of the project.

What should the manager DO at each stage?

Each stage in the evolution of the team from tentativeness to high performance requires a different response from the project manager.

The Tentative Stage

At this stage you as project manager should assume that your team are a team in name only, and your focus as manager should be on moving them on from this phase.

Actions you can take to do this include:

→ Recognise the need to move quickly out of this stage

→ Clarify the project aims and objectives

→ Set out goals, and discuss them at length - if they are not clear and accepted by everybody, the chances of team success are limited

→ Address concerns about Safety and Inclusion. Recognise that team members may well be asking themselves questions such as :

  - Why am I here?

  - What is my role?

  - What is expected of me?

  Make sure that you provide opportunities for discussion on these and other questions, both with the team and with individuals

→ Recognise the level of

dependency on the designated leader (You!)

→ Begin to create structure in the team, for example by an initial assignment of tasks based on each team member's skills.

The Assertive Stage

This is a critical stage. Failure to deal effectively with emerging tensions can lead the team into a downward spiral of conflict. Some of the actions the project manager should consider at this stage are:

→ Set team time to discuss process issues; time spent on resolving issues at this early stage will pay off later. Reviews and de-briefs on the initial tasks undertaken by the team members are an ideal starting point

→ Encourage talk about project goals and individual roles and responsibilities; listen to the team members, seek and accept their feedback and encourage them to do the same with each other

→ Be positive in setting out your vision for the project — "we can succeed"

→ Seek buy-in to objectives and activities

→ Seek early wins and acknowledge them

→ Take every opportunity to articulate the standards of performance and behaviour that you, as manager, expect from the team members.

The Normative Stage

Managing this stage effectively will steer the team towards deeper understanding of project goals and lay the basis for a solid team spirit. Actions the project manager should consider at this stage include:

→ Communicate constantly

→ Make norms of behaviour and performance explicit

→ Acknowledge achievements and link them to project goals

→ Recognise and acknowledge team-supportive behaviours

→ Delegate

→ Consult

→ Give regular feedback to individuals

→ Discuss process issues regularly with the team.

The Productive Stage

The manager's task at this stage is to maintain commitment to the conclusion of the project, and to avoid becoming complacent or getting stuck in a rut. Among the methods that could be considered are:

→ Agreeing stretch goals with individuals and team

→ Giving and receiving regular feedback on performance

→ Emphasising quality and attention to detail in its work

→ Ensuring the team takes time to evaluate its performance; both in terms of content (what we have been doing) and process (how well we are doing it)

→ Celebrate the achievement of project milestones.

The Final Stage

There is a fifth stage which should also be acknowledged - the end of the project. This can be something of an anti-climax, as the enthusiasm that has been generated among the team is dissipated. It is a good idea to mark the end of the project with an appropriate team event, which will give the team members a sense of closure, reinforce what they have learned (technical/professional/personal development) and encourage them in their careers.

Dealing with changes over the course of the Project

There is an important implication in the stages of team performance that we have discussed. Changes in the team - such as revised project objectives, changes in team personnel, a new team leader - will inevitably mean that the team will revert in some degree to the earlier stages as they come to terms with the new situation. It is important that managers realise that changes will require them to revisit the discussion and negotiation of the Assertive and Normative stages as the team comes to terms with the new situation. This means that there will be an inevitable 'blip' in the team's performance as it takes stock of its new situation. Of course the degree to which this occurs will vary depending on the team and their manager, but team managers should be aware that it is a factor and plan accordingly.

Panel 6.3

Developing the Mission Statement

Clarity about the project objective is an important factor in facilitating the progress of a team through the stages that lead to full effectiveness. It is particularly important in the initial phases of Tentativeness and Assertiveness that the project manager is able to articulate and explain the objective and link it to the role and contribution of each team member.

In doing this, some managers find that having a team Mission Statement can be useful. This typically takes the form of a brief and pithy summary of the project aims: What we want to achieve and how we intend to achieve it. It can include Project Objectives, Standards, Expectations, Boundaries & Limitations, and Values.

Team Guidelines

The same can be said of Behavioural Guidelines — whether or not to employ them is a judgement call that depends on the particular circumstances of the team.

Team ground-rules formalise the basis on which team members should work together to deal with issues of potential conflict or ambiguity for them. Examples could include:

→ **Scheduling:** *When to meet, how long, attendance, timekeeping*

→ **Procedures:** *Planning, scheduling, decision making*

→ **Participation:** *Everybody's views valued*

→ **Discussion:** *Listen, no interruptions, one voice at a time*

→ **Routine chores:** *Fair scheduling*

→ **Non-Team behaviour:** *Poor attitude, performance, behaviour, language.*

Examples of Team Ground rules

→ *Team problems are everybody's responsibility*

→ *Team time belongs to the team*

→ *Cultural tolerance — but not at the expense of standards*

→ *Don't talk about team members behind their backs*

→ *Don't speak negatively about competitors*

→ *Don't criticise ourselves externally*

→ *Don't promote hidden agendas.*

Sustaining Commitment over the life of the Project

Having attained the Productive stage, with a high level of commitment to the project deliverables and a clear objective and time line, it could be expected that the team would self-sustain high performance to the end. However, project managers cannot take this for granted; so they must develop a management style that provides appropriate leadership to a team of committed specialists, monitors their performance and intervenes when necessary. This is a task requiring some considerable finesse.

The project manager can sustain a culture of high performance through attention to the following factors:

❶ Clarity about the project objective

Keep focused on the deliverables. Project objectives evolve and change over the course of the project. The manager should ensure that all team members — who may be working on individual elements of the project without a clear overview of the total situation — are regularly briefed on the 'big picture'.

❷ Active participation of all members and information freely shared

Communication is the lifeblood of any team, and it is the manager's responsibility to ensure a free flow throughout the team. This involves ensuring that technical information is disseminated through appropriate groupware, and that the team members are convened regularly for opportunities for face-to-face communication.

❸ Issues confronted and dealt with openly

Conflict in the team is ok and members should feel free to openly express assertive or negative feelings — but winners or losers should be avoided. When conflict surfaces, the manager must ensure it is handled in a healthy manner, with the emphasis on project related matters, avoiding personality issues — keep the person and the problem separate.

❹ High level of trust between members, who support each other

Trust builds up during the evolution of the team, from its tentative phase, and the performance phase should be characterised by a high level of mutual trust. If anything happens to upset that trust — a dishonest action, a confidence betrayed, a commitment not met — all the good work of building the relationship can be put at nought and it can be difficult to retrieve the situation, especially in a project environment.

⑤ Sound and understood procedures for problem solving and decision making

How decisions are made and problems are solved is ultimately a question for the manager, who has a range of options from unilateral management decision-making to full autonomy delegated to the team. The important point to be stressed here is that the mode of decision making and the rationale for it should be clearly communicated and explained to the team.

⑥ Regular reviews of operations and learning from experience

The review of progress in both content and process should be a regular feature of the project. The practical way of achieving this is to schedule a review session on a regular basis within team meetings.

⑦ Celebrate performance and success

Marking significant project milestones, or the particular performance of individuals, helps sustain team commitment. It can be done in a variety of ways, but should be seen as sincere and thoughtful, rather than routine or formulaic

Summary of Chapter 6

→ Project team members take time to get to know one another

→ Making teams effective requires:

  - Attention to Process

  - Communicating effectively

  - Building and Maintaining cohesion

  - Establishing norms of behaviour

  - Transparent problem solving and decision making

  - Good leadership

→ Project managers should vary their behaviour relative to the development stages of a team

→ Handling changes during the project is a key skill

→ Project managers should work hard at creating and sustaining momentum

7 Leading an Effective Project Team

Chapter outline
Leading an Effective Project Team

→ The Nature of Team Leadership
→ Leadership for High Performance
→ Encouraging High Performance
→ Leadership in Practice - Making
   Meetings Effective
→ Delegated roles for Project Team
   Meetings
→ Disruptive Behaviour at Meetings
→ Managing Individual Team Members

The Nature of Team Leadership

The project manager acts as director, organiser and allocator of work and resources, ultimately accountable for delivery, and thus in overall control of the project.

Team leadership involves a parallel set of skills, embracing the roles of facilitator, motivator, delegator, coach and communicator, also comfortable with relying on the expertise of team members rather than being an expert in all aspects of the project.

This is a challenging set of requirements for the project manager. The figure below illustrates a contingency approach to team leadership. The manager has a range of options along a continuum from *direction* — where the manager makes the decision — to *delegation* — where the team has full responsibility. The choice is based on the manager's judgement regarding the competence of the team in the particular circumstances. This implies that the leadership role moves along the continuum, depending on circumstances.

Implicit in the model is the need for openness and two-way communication within the team so that the manager's decision as to leadership is discussed and understood.

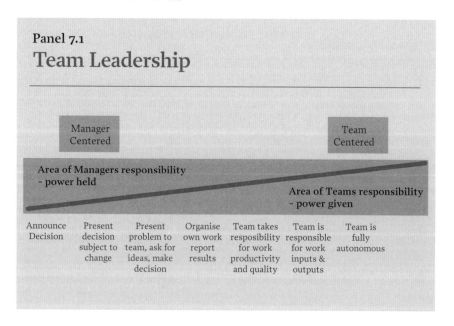

Panel 7.1

Team Leadership

Manager Centered						Team Centered

Area of Managers responsibility - power held

Area of Teams responsibility - power given

| Announce Decision | Present decision subject to change | Present problem to team, ask for ideas, make decision | Organise own work report results | Team takes resposibility for work productivity and quality | Team is responsible for work inputs & outputs | Team is fully autonomous |

Leadership for High Performance

Project teams are made up of competent individuals. Being a member of a project team can be a career enhancing opportunity. Team leaders should emphasise the opportunity and challenge by:

→ Encouraging team members to achieve their personal goals

→ Being a role model for high standards and values

→ Being clear about the performance and behaviour that you expect

→ Taking a stand on those issues you judge are key to project success

→ Confronting problems promptly

→ Being decisive

Encouraging High Performance

Many years of research and practice have taught managers that people can be motivated to a high level of performance when they:

→ Have clear and agreed goals, particularly if they help set those goals

→ Can see that their effort will produce useful results

→ Have a basis for positive envisioning of success

→ Get honest, open and regular feedback on their performance

The team building processes discussed in the preceding chapter provide the basis for implementing these principles. In addition, during the early stages of the project, project managers should give attention to the individual team members by:

→ Taking time to discuss project goals with individual team members, making clear how their role contributes to the project success, and

→ Encouraging individuals to link their role on the project to their career development − knowing that their contribution to the project will add value to their CV can be a major motivator for team members.

As the project proceeds, the manager must systematically follow through to ensure that the project plan is being implemented. At each major milestone, the manager should include:

→ Reviewing deliverables with each team member

→ Acknowledging successes

→ Getting commitment to corrective action if deliverables fall short

→ Encouraging each team member to generate improvement opportunities

→ Reinforcing communication of project goals, and performance standards.

Leadership in Practice - Making Meetings Effective

A critical area for any team leader is to manage meetings in a business like manner. This is particularly the case for project managers, where time will be at a premium, project deadlines pressing and team members will have a limited amount of time to devote to meetings. Yet the meeting is an essential means of progressing the project and of consolidating team performance.

Good meetings can be opportunities to promote teamwork, solve problems and keep the individual team members focused and motivated.

Making meetings effective and productive is a four-stage process.

Stage 1 - Preparation

Perhaps the leader's most important task is to ensure that the meeting has a clear purpose. This in turn determines the appropriate attendees.

Map out the steps needed to achieve the objectives and deliverables of the meeting, and make sure that any 'resources' needed (previous decisions, reports) will be available.

The team leader must also ensure adequate notice of the meeting, including venue and agenda, is circulated to all attendees.

Stage 2 - Starting the meeting

A business-like meeting should start on time; allowing slippage on start time will reward latecomers and establish a bad habit. The manager should welcome the participants, state the purpose of the meeting and clarify the critical procedures, especially the decision making process that will be followed.

Stage 3 - During the meeting

Key points for the project manager are:

→ keep to time

→ encourage communication

→ keep to the point

→ summarise progress

→ record decisions.

Finally, when the technical issues on the agenda are dealt with, it is good practice to take some time to review process issues — that is, how they are performing as a team, and this is an opportunity for two-way communication between project manager and the team.

Stage 4 - Ending

Summarise what has been agreed, set date for next meeting and thank the participants.

Delegated roles for Project Team Meetings

While the project manager has a leadership responsibility to ensure project meetings are run on a business like basis, some aspects of the meeting process can be delegated.

There are a number of roles which contribute to an effective meeting that can, and should, be delegated to team members on a rotating basis. These are:

The Co-ordinator

→ Keeps the process focused & moving

→ Encourages full participation

→ Leads reviews and summarises

This is often assumed to be the team leader's role, but can be delegated.

The Timekeeper

→ Watches the clock

→ Assigns a time to each agenda item, and reminds the meeting as time passes

→ Gets agreement on re-allocation of time if an agenda item goes over time

→ Ensures meeting finishes on time.

The Scribe

→ Records key information

→ Clarifies/illuminates the process

→ Distributes meeting reports.

Panel 7.2

Recording a meeting

Recording the proceedings of a meeting does not imply keeping detailed minutes of all contributions. What is required is a record of what was agreed, who is responsible for delivery and by when.

This can be done on a flip chart, as set out below. This has the added advantage of providing a visual record of progress on the agenda items

Agenda Item	Decision	Action and Responsibility	Date Due
1			
2			
3			
4			
5			

The Gatekeeper

→ Manages interruptions, liaises with outside.

Disruptive Behaviour at Meetings

There are a variety of behaviours that can disrupt a meeting. Here is a representative sample, with an indication of what the team leader might consider doing in each case:

The 'Silent Type': a team member who is not contributing to the meeting. The team leader can invite them to comment, ask a direct question, or simply ask them to confirm that they are happy with the tone and direction of the meeting.

The 'Talker': a team member who monopolises the debate. The leader can invite others to join in, or tackle the person directly.

The 'Wanderer': whose contributions are irrelevant to the topic.

In circumstances such as these the leader should intervene to cut short irrelevant contributions, which waste time and irritate other team members. It may be necessary to speak to the individual one-on-one after the meeting.

Separate meetings: if two or more team members begin a conversation while the meeting is in progress, the leader should intervene immediately, with a comment such as "one voice at a time please".

The meeting is floundering: the leader can restate the objective, set new goals, or ask challenging questions.

When the meeting is deadlocked: acknowledge the difficulty, review the facts, re-state the issues or call a recess for one-on-one discussions.

Dissention: if a team member is strongly disagreeing consider shifting the argument to somebody else, if the person has a good point, re-open an analysis of the issue.

In most cases, project managers will find themselves dealing with competent and committed individuals, anxious for success and willing to do their best.

Managing Individual Team Members

In most cases, project managers will find themselves dealing with competent and committed individuals, anxious for success and willing to do their best. In these circumstances, milestone reviews and feedback sessions will be task focused business-like and a positive experience for all concerned.

Occasionally however, project managers will be faced with a team member whose performance or behaviour is, for some reason, giving cause for concern. In these cases, the project manager has to decide on the appropriate intervention – should the matter be referred to the individual's line manager, or dealt with at project level.

If the latter, good practice stresses that project managers should ensure any critical feedback is:

→ Timely: *Appreciation of good performance should be shown as soon as possible. If there are problems they should also be discussed as soon as possible. Team members should not go for long periods thinking they are doing well when they are not - or vice versa*

→ Concise and specific

→ Honest

→ Appropriately given; *Critical feedback should always be given in private*

→ Behaviourally based and Objective: *Based on fact & evidence rather than judgemental*

The project manager should also recognise that best practice guidelines suggests that she/he should:

→ Give information in manageable amounts

→ Check perception and understanding regularly during the discussion

→ Ensure your feedback has been accurately and clearly understood

→ Focus on issues the person can do something about

→ Clarify your expectations & explore solutions

→ If leaving them with a choice make sure they are aware of consequences.

Summary of Chapter 7

→ Choose project team leadership style appropriate to team competence

→ Delegate some leadership responsibilities to the team

→ Develop as much as possible a high level of trust between team members

→ Work hard at achieving high performance from individuals and team, principally through goal setting and feedback

→ Utilise best practice to optimise effectiveness of meetings

→ Actively manage disruptive behaviour at meetings

→ Celebrate mini-success and overall success.

8 Managing Stakeholders

Chapter outline
Managing Stakeholders

"All know the way; few actually walk it."

Bodhidharma

→   Key steps in Managing Stakeholders
→   Classifying Stakeholders
→   Identifying Stakeholder Groups
→   Assessing Stakeholder Interest
     and Activism
→   Recognising different Stakeholder
     Types based on Power Legitimacy
     and Urgency
→   Mapping Stakeholder Resistance
→   Dealing with Irrational Stakeholder
     Activity
→   Managing 'Needs' and 'Wants'
→   Role of the Sponsor
→   Exploring Scope, Expressed Needs and
     Latent Desires
→   Success and Failure: Managing
     Reality & Perception
→   Delivering Bad News on a Project
→   Delivering Good News on a Project

Key Steps in Managing Stakeholders

Managing stakeholders (their perceptions, needs and desires) is a crucial but elusive aspect of project management. Stakeholder management not only addresses the actual needs and latent wants of the various stakeholders, but forms a strategy for effective communications and indeed political collaboration in a project.

Panel 8.1

Key steps in managing stakeholders

→ Identify potential stakeholders, including non-obvious influencers

→ Understand their stated and hidden interests, legitimate or not

→ Assess their power and willingness to use that power

→ Identify the likely coalitions they might form

→ Consider stakeholder strengths and weaknesses

→ Identify strategies and predict stakeholder responses

→ Form appropriate action plans

→ Communicate actively with stakeholders

Classifying Stakeholders

A stakeholder is a person or group with an effective interest or stake in a project; the interest can be used positively or negatively.

Stakeholders are generally treated as individuals or groups of similar interest, but in practice they can be a shifting web of influences and interests.

Stakeholders are not all equal in power or identical in interest; some indirect stakeholders, such as regulatory agencies, may not be true enablers but may instead be powerful stumbling blocks unless certain standards or criteria are met.

Identifying Stakeholder Groups

Typical primary stakeholders include investors, clients, customers, purchasers, users, department heads and other executives. The range of stakeholders can be surprisingly large, as illustrated below, with many holding enough power to delay or even derail a project.

Projects can be impacted by the influence of critical gate-holders whose approval must be obtained, such as regulators, as well as custodians who restrict access to key decision makers. There are also myriad guardian groups who seek to preserve sectional interests, cliques of various kinds, committee chairpersons of various types, and those who control the channels of communication; personal assistants, receptionists, or family members. These all can exert real influence and must be treated accordingly.

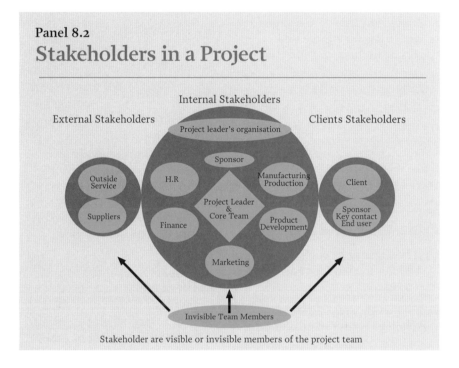

Panel 8.2

Stakeholders in a Project

Stakeholder are visible or invisible members of the project team

Assessing Stakeholder Interests and Activism

Stakeholder groups can initially be assessed in terms of their power (current and potential) and their 'stake' in the project's outcomes, as shown below:

	High Stake or Importance	Low Stake or Importance
High Influence / Power	**Critical stakeholder group** Collaborate with these	**Useful for opinion forming** Reduce impact
Low Influence / Power	**Important group** Empower & involve	**Low priority stakeholders** Monitor or ignore

A third dimension can be added, that of politics and persuasion. This is the propensity to pursue one's case, whether legitimate or not, and requires a willingness to use whatever power and means available.

Recognising different Stakeholder Types based on Power, Legitimacy and Urgency

Stakeholders differ in respect of three key elements:

1. Their willingness to use power

2. The legitimacy of their claims

3. The urgency or energy with which they pursue those claims.

Consequently, eight different stakeholder types can be identified:

1. Dormant stakeholders (Power, no legitimacy and no urgency)

2. Discretionary stakeholders (Legitimacy, but no power and no urgency)

3. Demanding stakeholders (Urgency, but no legitimacy and no power)

4. Dominant stakeholders (Power and legitimacy, but no urgency)

5. Dangerous stakeholders (Power and urgency, but no legitimacy)

6. Dependent stakeholders (Legitimacy and urgency, but no power)

7. Definitive stakeholders (Power, legitimacy and urgency)

8. Non-stakeholders (No power, no legitimacy and no urgency)

Dormant stakeholders are an untapped source of power for the project leader; they can be activated through increasing their awareness of the situation and through appeals to their self-interest.

Discretionary stakeholders lack power but can be stimulated to press the legitimacy of their interests, especially if the project leader can facilitate them, and especially if they can be united to act in a concerted manner.

Demanding stakeholders create a nuisance, stridently pressing illegitimate claims; placate such groups and make minor concessions to secure accord.

Dominant stakeholders have power and legitimacy but are not actively pursuing their interests; rational persuasion and increased awareness can bring this vital group to more active involvement, especially if the cost to them of non-involvement is highlighted.

Dangerous stakeholders have power and are actively pressing invalid claims; their influence can be reduced by revealing the illegitimate nature of their claims, by invoking the power of other stakeholders or senior management and by forming coalitions.

Dependent stakeholders are often beneficiaries of the project but lack power because they are solitary and voiceless; work to unite such groups and articulate their claims.

Definitive stakeholders are demanding, legitimate and active, and should be central to any stakeholder management strategy; treat these with respect and integrity.

Mapping Stakeholder Resistance

An initial appraisal of stakeholder 'needs and wants' can be combined with an assessment of their resistance. This will help develop a picture of the feasibility and political viability of the project proposal. It can be also be used to identify sources of resistance and critical stakeholders, to generate ways to weaken opposition, to strengthen supporting forces and indeed to suggest what coalitions might prove effective.

Take for example a proposal to extend a golf course in the suburbs. Although generally welcome, the proposal meets fierce opposition from dedicated lobby groups. Environmentalists want more green space but are ideologically committed to resisting the use of pesticides. When it is discovered that the fairway skirts a ruined castle opposition from heritage groups becomes heightened. The local council asserts its authority though a series of planning permission restrictions. The Golfing Union is officially in favour, but actually resents the course expansion.

Local residents are split in their support and level of activism; while the golf course extension provides high amenity value, it also brings some safety issues (from errant golf shots) and extra traffic. It should be noted that such support is tacit and unassertive, while opposition is active, vocal and committed. This is a typical conundrum for project managers: support is passive, opposition is aggressive, and inertia seeks to preserve the status quo.

Mapping the stakeholders, and evaluating the extent of their active resistance or support produces a 'Force-field Analysis'; weak forces are rated low ('1' on the scale), moderate forces are rated 2 or 3, but sustained strong resistance is rated as a negative force vector, shown as '- 5' over leaf:

Panel 8.3

Project Stakeholders

	Who are the Stake-holders?	What do they say they want?	What are really their needs?	Rate their degree of influence	
				Can Impede	Can Help
1				-5 -4 -3 -2 -1	0 1 2 3 4 5
2				-5 -4 -3 -2 -1	0 1 2 3 4 5
3				-5 -4 -3 -2 -1	0 1 2 3 4 5
4				-5 -4 -3 -2 -1	0 1 2 3 4 5
5				-5 -4 -3 -2 -1	0 1 2 3 4 5
6				-5 -4 -3 -2 -1	0 1 2 3 4 5
7				-5 -4 -3 -2 -1	0 1 2 3 4 5
8				-5 -4 -3 -2 -1	0 1 2 3 4 5

It can quickly be noted that key stakeholders had been omitted such as green-keepers, who would benefit from the project, a powerful local hotelier who might benefit, groups looking to engage local youths in sport, and a newly-arrived bank manager keen to join the club.

Anticipating little chance of changing the environmentalist and heritage lobby groups, the dormant and latent forces must be energised, the quieter voices amplified, lethargic groups activated, and coalitions formed.

Ultimately, the project succeeds, by two further measures: changing the timing of the project until an upcoming election to gain enough political support, and, crucially, by creating a bogeyman strategy - leaking 'news' that the land could now be sold for high-density development. Faced with this alternative, resistance weakened and permission was obtained.

Dealing with Irrational Stakeholder Activity

In assessing stakeholder reaction, it can be useful to consider, along with their degree of antagonism, the stakeholder's propensity to negotiate, as opposed to play to win at any cost. Those conscious of their power, but with no personal axe to grind, will usually negotiate. Those personally antagonistic will be prepared to act more dangerously; these types must be dealt with at the emotional as well as the rational level.

Managing 'Needs' and 'Wants'

A *'need'* can be considered an essential aspect or function that the project is expected to deliver, such as a brochure (for a company about to market its products) or a well-attended event (for a customer promoting a new service). Not meeting these 'needs' is clearly a failure but ironically not meeting some particular 'wants' of a client can result in a severe, personalised reaction.

A 'want' can be an aspect, not strictly essential, that appeals to a client's ego or has some other emotional value. For example, if a client is using this brochure for self-publicity or for reflected glory, failure to deliver on any aspect can result in disproportionate reaction and consequences for the project manager.

In many cases, it is actually better to satisfy ego aspects first, if possible, as this provides a stronger emotional basis for a relationship.

It is invariably worthwhile to take the time to develop a detailed scope document at the beginning of any project to manage expectations. The key is to probe client needs by exploring the plan, assessing the cost, effort, benefits, constraints and risks of the project. This encourages both you and the client to think through the elements of the project or request, and helps reveal the true interpretation of the planned work.

Role of the Sponsor

Although it is a cliché that effective sponsorship is crucial for success, the role of the sponsor is often under-developed. As well as authorising and underwriting a project, the effective sponsor supports the project leader politically, mentors the project leader on occasion and provides a strategic perspective to the project leader.

In complex organisations, where, for example, several division heads are required to contribute project team members, they may:

→ send their least effective people

→ send people simply as representatives looking out solely for their division's interests or

→ they may deliberately undermine a project. In these cases, a project manager will need the political support and practical assistance of a senior executive. The sponsor also helps by channelling news and by presenting the project in a positive light as needed.

Managing Upwards

Actively cultivate relationships with senior staff. Go the extra mile in producing reports, for example. Build relationships in advance by seeking out meetings with influential stakeholders. Show your value by providing scarce information or contributing new ideas. Network with a variety of potentially influential executives. Host opinion forums and invite special guest speakers. Work to make your relationships with higher-level stakeholders more equal and less dependent.

Managing Multiple or Conflicting Needs

Where there are multiple needs, solutions will have to be explored more fully, as more complicated trade-offs are involved. Indeed, where conflicting needs emerge, this results in a true dilemma.

For example, a project may entail designing a component that is both strong and light. These are contending opposites, but the dilemma can be resolved by using lightweight alloys (a more expensive solution) or changing the shape of the piece to give more strength (with some additional design expense).

Success and Failure: Managing Reality & Perception

Exploring Scope, Expressed Needs and Latent Desires

The expressed need frequently understates or even obscures the actual need. For example, a highly regarded engineering colleague was asked to manage a project to establish a second factory in a large existing facility. The expressed need was stated in engineering and construction terms such as plant size and machines required.

The colleague realised that the unstated need was for a highly productive factory that excelled in all aspects, including organisational aspects such as a culture of employee engagement with high productivity standards, flexible work scheduling and task multi-skilling.

The engineering specification was necessary but not sufficient for the true purpose; he set about working with staff of all levels to design a facility that worked for people as well as machines. Employees became part of the design team, and influenced such decisions as work flow, layout, process monitoring, team flexibility and even break times. They took ownership for the design, and its subsequent flawless operation. Union issues melted away and the climate became highly collaborative. The sense of pride in the facility was palpable. Petty grievances were resolved, systems were streamlined and, naturally, productivity and innovation exceeded all expectations. Factories are not just buildings; they are living communities.

Limiting scope is a good maxim, as it simplifies the project and reduces the potential for risk, but in this case meeting only the expressed need for a factory would have been insufficient.

The engineer's career progressed rapidly on account of the acumen and range of skills demonstrated. In this case, unleashing the spirit of employees, some of whom had been expressing their frustration in destructive ways, caused productivity to flourish. Their sense of pride in the final design was palpable.

In many cases 'perception is reality' and so perceptions must be actively managed.

For example, an office move might be successful in that all the equipment was correctly installed, but if the real goal was

a more productive layout (or the dismantling of established cliques, or the improvement in communications between departments) then the move may be perceived only as a limited success.

This perception, although unfair, may be covertly transmitted along the office grapevine, harming the project leader's reputation. Better to explore latent needs and to precisely agree the true deliverables. Otherwise the goals are so obscured that the project manager is working blind.

Managing expectations starts with setting goals and extends to shaping attitudes towards the effort, risks and rewards involved; try to under-promise and over-deliver, so that expectations are exceeded.

Delivering Bad News on a Project

"Every project looks like a failure in the middle"

Rosabeth Moss Kanter

Almost every project will have setbacks that need to be communicated expertly. In giving such news, it is advisable to prepare well to lessen the impact by bringing perspective on the scale of the setback. Remedies and mitigating solutions should also be proposed.

Deliver bad news in a single dose

To paraphrase Machiavelli, bad news should be delivered all at once. A constant drip of negative news is debilitating, and it reflects poorly on those managing the project. Where possible, suggest measures to alleviate the situation. Bad news should be accompanied by an explanation, an apology, and a promise of better things to come.

Preparing the ground

Recalling project successes can build a safer platform from which to deliver bad news.

Having a track record of success, meeting deadlines and delivering on promises (even minor ones) can be presented as evidence of capability and trustworthiness.

Build relationships and have support in place before you ever need it.

Make prior project achievements visible, and call on support from sponsors and peers.

The impact of your bad news can be softened by adopting a calm demeanor; the right tone can promote harmony, but shrill notes strike the wrong chord.

Contrast the news with the many successes the project has enjoyed, and bring whatever alternatives or counter-measures you can muster.

Use any planned contingencies

A proper risk analysis will have signaled the dangers well in advance.

If you have had the foresight to negotiate contingency arrangements, use those arrangements now.

Try to offset shortcomings in one phase by wringing gains out of later activities.

Use your network to discover possible ways to recover the situation.

Leverage opportunities to recover losses. Revisit the scope so that the overall project can succeed.

Delivering Good News on a Project

Project managers or their team often do not get the credit their efforts deserve. Good news, such as the early completion of a milestone, may even invoke suspicions that the schedule was padded. Place good news in context, gift-wrap it and deliver the glad tidings only when the timing is right.

Good news is rarely urgent, and so should never be rushed. Promote project successes subtly, in understated ways.

Use a wide variety of means; bad news will travel fast on its own accord.

Deliver good news often, without seeking to take the credit

personally; let your team take the credit, and your graciousness will be repaid, many times over.

Note that success in a project can be surprisingly hard to judge; so indeed can failure.

Summary of Chapter 8

→ Help ensure project success by understanding stakeholders' motivations

→ Leverage stakeholder wants for overall satisfaction with the project

→ Deliver on actual needs to produce value

→ Consciously manage perceptions; broadcast project successes discreetly

→ Actively promote the project and recruit, rather than just enlist, stakeholders

→ Deliver bad news only after setting the scene; put matters in perspective

→ Seize the initiative by actively managing your boss and other senior stakeholders

→ Gift wrap good news and deliver when timing is right

"We are what we think. All that we are, arises from our thoughts. With our thoughts we make the world"

Guatama Buddha
(560-477 BC)

9 Managing Costs

Chapter outline
Managing Costs

"A fool knows the price of everything but the value of nothing."

Proverb

→ Recognising Distortions that affect Project Cost Accounting
→ Developing a System to Track and Control Costs
→ Using the Earned Value System to understand Actual Costs and Progress
→ Recovering Project Cost Over-spend
→ Noting early Cost Discrepancies and their Causes
→ Managing Risks by Developing Contingency Plans and Budgets

Recognising Distortions that affect Project Cost Accounting

Although cost considerations are invariably paramount, it can be difficult to forecast and control project costs accurately. This is because of the 'once-off' nature of projects and the time delays between performing work and accounting for that work. The prediction, tracking and controlling of costs do not receive proper attention and this results in unexpected costs, budget shortfalls and compromised quality.

The true cost implications of decisions made early in the project, especially in the design stage, may not become evident until later in the project. Similarly, the opportunity to affect cost decreases as the project progresses.

Panel 9.1

Distortions in Cost Management

→ the delayed nature of recognising costs can distort the value of work performed

→ the uncertainty of knowing if work was performed satisfactorily

→ the effect on cost of scope creep, changes to the plan or schedule

→ rework, unplanned expenditures and emergencies

→ late ('after-the-fact') purchase orders and unauthorised expenditures

→ lack of visibility of on-going fixed costs, such as project support cost

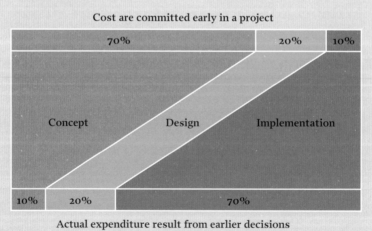

Cost are committed early in a project

| 70% | 20% | 10% |

Concept · Design · Implementation

| 10% | 20% | 70% |

Actual expenditure result from earlier decisions

Figure: Decisions made early in the project lifecycle determine later costs

A complicating factor in managing project cost is the delay between the execution of work and the subsequent invoicing and payment for that work, which means that accounting delays can distort the visibility of project costs.

Additionally, work may not be properly performed, the scope may change and material prices can easily fluctuate. The emphasis therefore must be on identifying early any variations in both the work performed and the cost (or value) arising.

As a design engineering manager for a telecommunications manufacturer, the temptation was to reduce my own department's costs by prematurely declaring designs complete; this would have been a false economy, as the consequences are significant and costly.

Developing a System to Track and Control Costs

The basic step in budgeting and tracking costs is to attach the relevant costs, such as time or material costs, to each task in the Work Breakdown Structure, described on Page 23. The WBS provides a hierarchical framework of tasks to which unique identifying cost codes can be attached. These costs can then be tracked to the lowest level, the task 'package'.

External costs, such as contractor charges, equipment hire or machinery purchases can be subsequently controlled by having signature authority on approval of Purchase Orders, Work Orders and the like.

Note that further adjustments need to be made for conditional costs such as bonuses, discounts or rebates.

Internal project support costs can be managed using a simple tracking system, but take care to make this a simple, routine habit for all concerned.

Using the Earned Value System to understand Actual Costs and Progress

The key is to realise that costs taken in isolation from planned and actual outcomes can be misleading. In these cases, the actual *'earned value'* must be determined to identify the extent of the cost slippage, as distinct to schedule slippage.

Consider the situation where, at the mid-point time of the project, expenditures are 10% less than planned. This can be due to positive aspects such as excellent negotiation or unexpectedly high productivity. Equally it could be due to unexpectedly favourable conditions, simple good fortune or excessively padded cost estimates.

Frequently, the lower than expected costs reveal that progress is actually seriously behind schedule, perhaps due to a late project start.

To compound matters, whatever progress that is made has come at the expense of costs higher than anticipated, perhaps due to additional payments made to recover the slippage in the schedule.

For these reasons, *'earned value'* cost management techniques track expenditures versus planned and actual achievements over time rather than relying on simple aggregated costs.

In the chart below, the middle line is the planned budget baseline, while the upper line reflects the actual costs incurred. In contrast, the lower line shows actual accomplishment, the value said to be earned by the work delivered. In this illustration, there is a large discrepancy, indicating that the project is both late and over budget.

Panel 9.2

Progress Against Plan

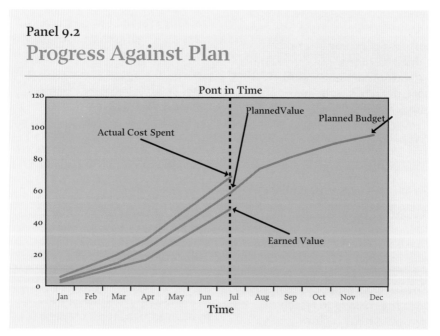

Recovering Project Cost Over-spend

Recovering cost over-runs is difficult but can be achieved by reducing project scope, omitting aspects of the project and negotiating lower costs with the remaining items.

Cutting features, using cheaper grade materials, reducing safety margins, substituting cheaper alternatives, short-changing contractors and reneging on contracts are all common but unethical ploys, done surreptitiously.

It is invariably better and more productive to seek genuine savings through real problem-solving, gain-sharing and joint negotiation.

The project manager may have unusual sources of power in these negotiations: she may be able, for example, to advance the project quicker, and allow earlier use of the deliverables to gain additional revenue for the client.

The project manager may conversely be able to re-negotiate costs if the client makes specification changes. The project manager could increase bargaining power by creating value in other ways, for example, by identifying new commercial opportunities or delivering an unexpected project benefit.

> The project manager may conversely be able to re-negotiate costs if the client makes specification changes.

Cost over-runs are sometimes allowed in a project, especially where the cost increases are outside the project's control e.g. certain raw materials, such as oil, and other traded commodities fluctuate over time. It is useful to negotiate these at the outset: as a minimum, it highlights to the client some hidden risks and potential liabilities you are absorbing, and you may also even wring some concessions.

Note that budgets should have a tolerance for *uncertainty,* as well as contingency *budgets against specific risks.* Budget 'allowances' are specific amounts allowed in the budget to deal with the fact that estimates cannot always be precise. They are forecasts that represent a likely budgeted figure somewhere along the true spectrum of costs.

Noting early Cost Discrepancies and their Causes

It is worth noting that cost and schedule overruns in the early stages of a project invariably become amplified as the project progresses. If the first milestone has such problems, it can be worthwhile to re-examine the project's assumptions, and especially to check the basis for estimation used to identify systemic errors.

Use the initial project stages to check if your control mechanisms are capable of detecting and signalling cost problems.

The goal, of course, is to bring the project to successful completion, and it is essential to re-plan by forecasting the Expected Cost to Completion over the remaining time. The overruns can often be brought back into line by re-negotiating contracts, reducing surplus features, lowering material grades or finding better methods. These can lead to innovative recovery programmes and smarter ways of working in the future. The chart below shows potential end cost and completion dates. Note these re-planned projections are higher than originally budgeted but will reduce the excessive over-runs and delays.

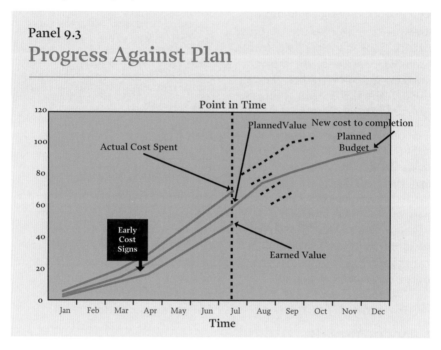

Panel 9.3

Progress Against Plan

It's content labels: Point in Time, PlannedValue, New cost to completion, Planned Budget, Actual Cost Spent, Early Cost Signs, Earned Value, Time

In the illustration, the divergence between the planned and actual costs can be discovered from the very beginning of the project.

It is essential that these early warning signs are used to discover the true cause of cost problems. These can be failures in execution or alternatively deficiencies in planning. Problems may be rooted in deeper causes such as low motivation, poor supervision or weak teamwork.

The soft issues are subtler to detect but can be uncovered by the project manager being approachable and receptive; enquire how people are coping with the tasks, probe emerging issues, discuss progress and simply be accessible. Prevent cost issues through better project briefings, conscious team formation and pre-emptive moves to defuse potential sources of conflict.

Managing Risks by Developing Contingency Plans and Budgets

Often, project budgets do not adequately allow for risks. Risks should be assigned an 'economic value' based on the cost consequences of that risk occurring and any amounts invested in risk prevention. In the following illustration, the revenues are regarded as having a 90% probability, but planned costs are regarded as essentially certain. Each significant risk is then evaluated for its economic outcomes, with probability ratings assigned. On the positive side, opportunities such as an additional revenue stream, are similarly factored into this *'utility chart'* to calculate the final *'expected monetary value'*.

Panel 9.4
Utility Chart - Expected Monetary Value Table

	Cost Impact € / $	Probability	EMV
Predicted Income	1000	90%	900
Expected Costs	-700	99%	-693
Risk / threat 1	-400	10%	-40
Risk / threat 2	-300	5%	-15
Opportunity 1	+200	20%	+40
Opportunity 2	+150	33%	+50
Net Expected Monetary Value			242

Finally, while cost is a major preoccupation for project managers, ultimately cost is secondary to quality: if the deliverables fail to meet requirements, it is pointless to highlight the cost savings.

"It's unwise to pay too much, but it's worse to pay too little. When you pay too much, you lose a little money, that is all. When you pay too little, you sometimes lose everything, because the thing you bought was incapable of doing the thing it was bought to do".

John Ruskin,
1819-1900.

Summary of Chapter 9

→ Manage costs from the outset by having a good budget and tracking system

→ Develop an early-warning cost prevention system

→ Use the baseline budget to monitor and control costs

→ Use earned value to assess true costs and progress in the project

→ Realise that an under-spend may conceal project slippage and hidden causes

→ Add cost allowances for unknown or uncertain elements in a project

→ Have an agreed contingency budget against specific risks occurring

→ Calculate the cost-to-completion as often as necessary

→ Know the expected monetary value and look for opportunities as well as risks.

Project Review – Capturing the Learning 10

Chapter outline
Project Review – Capturing the Learning

"Leadership and learning are indispensable to
 each other"

John F. Kennedy

→ Completing the Project
→ Planning the Project Review
→ Developing Team and Individual
   Learning Capability
→ Developing a Learning Cycle: the Power
   of Reflection and Feedback
→ Developing Real and Meaningful
   Dialogue
→ Deepening the Learning Cycle
→ Making Conversations Real and
   Meaningful
→ Reflection Stages

Completing the Project

Concluding a project demands attention to detail in solving the myriad seemingly-small details that prevent final approval. It also involves gleaning the lessons learned and disbanding the project team, both difficult activities. The key factor is to close the project so that it stays closed and doesn't persist interminably.

Panel 10.1

Post-Project Reviews - Aims

→ Capture lessons learned

→ Understand where knowledge, tacit and otherwise resides

→ Build organisational and project capabilities

→ Introduce and expand best practice

→ Build knowledge and skill bases

→ Develop a sense of community by developing best practice

→ Archive information and establish knowledge directories

→ Close the file on the project

"Learning in organisations means the continuous testing of experience, and the transformation

of that experience into knowledge - accessible to the whole organisation and relevant to its core purpose."

Peter Senge, 1990.

Planning the Project Review

Project reviews are frequently acrimonious. In order to avoid project reviews becoming bitter and frustrating, consider the following:

→ Assess the project, its methods and outcomes in a balanced way; do not sit in judgement, but recognise achievements, note contributions, praise exemplary behaviours and showcase positive factors.

→ Name sins, not sinners: if faults must be mentioned, avoid personalising the critique. Remember to praise in public but criticise only in private.

→ Use the project baseline as the basis for assessment: stick to the key facts, noting slippages, misconceptions, unrealistic planning assumptions, interface issues. Focus on undisputed measurements, based on agreed deliverables.

→ Do not use the final review as payback time, in which you get your revenge on those who have trespassed against you!

→ Minimise the extent and depth of the final project review by having a balanced assessment

91

incorporated into the earlier milestone reviews.

→ Use continuous assessment and stakeholder engagement so that there are no major surprises at the end. In a sense, there is little point of only having a review at the very end of a project, when it is too late for that project to benefit.

→ Build an atmosphere throughout the project where the team (including the other stakeholders) feels free to offer and accept constructive criticism; this is the high-performance stage for teams.

→ Celebrate often and well: a good party provides opportunity for re-creation and reconciliation. Use the opportunity to properly recognise notable contributions; invite senior management and key stakeholders to perform the ceremonies.

→ Take all the blame, but none of the credit, deserved or not.

→ Share the learning widely, use all means available, electronic and traditional.

→ Take time out and smell the roses.

Developing Team and Individual Learning Capability

It is wisely noted that while everybody wants to learn, few want to be taught; significant emotional barriers have to be overcome, because criticism potentially intrudes on an individual's self-esteem. Self-preservation is a strong instinct and public criticism raises the spectre of loss of reputation - losing 'face' is a universal human concern.

Ability to learn is hampered by the tacit nature of important information and perceptual differences when reviewing even seemingly 'hard' data.

In order to develop a high-performance team and have useful reviews, it is therefore necessary to:

→ instil a genuine desire for learning and development

→ promote an appetite for constructive criticism

→ secure a safe atmosphere, and

→ have a reliable review process that focuses on the project baseline.

Developing a Learning Cycle: the Power of Reflection and Feedback

The hallmark of successful individuals and teams is their ability to continually learn; that is, to actively seek feedback, discriminate between good and bad advice and then to act appropriately.

This involves a cyclical process of consciously and deliberately planning, taking action, evaluating that action, leading in turn to further planning. This learning cycle has four discernable stages:

❶ Experiencing and observing events

❷ Reflecting on root causes and observed outcomes

❸ Interpreting events and making the decision to act or not

❹ Taking purposeful action

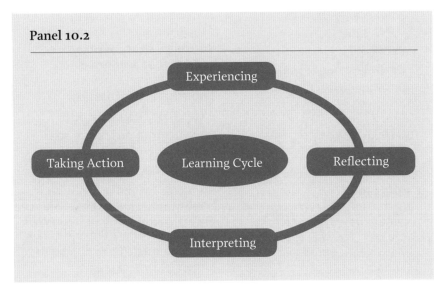

Panel 10.2

The cycle is repeated, and each cycle can yield improved results. The key individual barriers are self-imposed:

→ unwillingness to accept feedback,

→ denial of evidence,

→ distortion of facts,

→ reluctance to change, or

→ constant deferral of action.

Similarly, teams can:

→ attempt to shift blame,

→ indulge in inappropriate politics, and

→ refuse to accept feedback.

Examples of learning organisations are remarkably few, but organisations that rely on high performance and close co-ordination provide useful examples: rescue services, quick-response teams, crack military squads, airline crews.

Researchers analysing these situations realised that many tragic accidents arose, not from lack of information, but a reluctance to communicate that information upwards, for example, to the senior pilot. As these organisations are involved in life-or-death situations, failure is not an option; this has led to the development of learning as a habit, with explicit routines and clear expectations, as implied below.

→ Clear feedback will be given in a timely and relevant manner

→ Feedback upwards from lower ranks is explicitly required

→ De-briefings focus on facts, not personalities

→ How well was the team prepared?

→ Were the risks considered?

→ Were the response times adequate?

→ Were the correct signals used?

→ Were communication protocols utilised?

It is essential to avoid direct blame; individual performance must be addressed, but focus on future improvement rather than past failings. Such coaching can generate an appetite for reducing shortcomings. Focus on the original baseline plan, noting how the deficiencies emerged.

For example, the review could focus:

→ on the accuracy of the estimating

→ the logic of the scheduling

→ the availability of resources

→ the quality of communications

→ the degree of co-ordination

→ the control of costs, or

→ the ability to correct problems as they arise.

Done correctly, early milestone reviews can be crucial in delivering successful project outcomes in a challenging yet constructive manner.

Developing Real and Meaningful Dialogue

Conversations can often be mere social constructs, bounded by etiquette, essentially meaningless, designed to fill a vacuum. Real dialogue depends on mutual exploration of important issues in a constructive manner, and such dialogue is crucial to project performance.

The McKinsey View on Real Learning and Dialogue

'The nature of the conversations that take place in organisations, and the language used for those conversations, are important determinants of organisational success and distinctiveness. Much energy is put into building project lessons which provide an 'internal market-place' for readily accessible ideas, and experienced individual consultants act as mentors giving advice to other colleagues. Conversations are fundamental to McKinsey's functioning.'

Deepening the Learning Cycle

Often the real quest is not to find a better answer, but to find a better question that then can lead to discovery. Effective project leadership can entail creating space for reflection, for the individual and also for the team, especially if there are major changes to be addressed. By framing and re-framing the question, underlying factors can be revealed, creating new insights and different possibilities. Expanding the learning promotes deeper thinking and promotes more solutions:

"Where there is much desire to learn, there of necessity will be much arguing, much writing, many opinions, for opinions is but knowledge in the making." - John Milton, 1608-1674, English Poet.

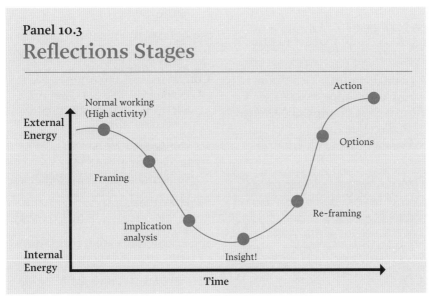

Panel 10.3
Reflections Stages

Actively circulate knowledge around the organisation, as it will benefit both the organisation and your team, while building your reputation for progressive management.

Making Conversations Real and Meaningful

"The first responsibility of a leader is to define reality" - Max dePree

This is not a licence for bluntness but encouragement to see and relate the actual situation, and to take appropriate action. Flexibility in style, to suit different personalities and different situations, is crucial to high performance and learning.

Project leadership focus can at one moment be on coaching for high performance, at another on being a guardian, protecting and

95

supporting, and yet another on tapping the network for resources; it can even have to shift to counselling in some cases.

In coaching mode, the project leader sets goals and acts as a critical friend, challenging and collaborating.

As a guardian, the leader protects, the behaviour of 'role-models'.

As a networker, the leader opens doors and facilitates change.

As a counsellor, the leader might actively listen and offer suggestions.

As a project progresses through its lifecycle, the appropriate style for effective leadership must change from directive through facilitative to collaborative.

> "Act as resources to each other, exchanging information, making sense of situations, sharing new tricks and ideas, as well as keeping each other company and spicing up each other's working days."
>
> P. Wenger,
> 1998.

Summary of Chapter 10

→ Learning and leading are complementary skills

→ A climate of learning can produce continuous improvement

→ Purposeful reflection and deliberate action produce a valuable learning habit

→ Develop the learning habit by conducting reviews from the earliest milestone

→ Use feedback as the 'breakfast of champions' to fuel learning and improvement

→ Make feedback constructive by assessing progress against the agreed baseline

→ Confidence breeds achievement, and vice versa; consciously nurture confidence

→ Have real conversations with much debate, and little rancour.

→ True leaders adjust their own style to suit others

"He who knows only his side of the case, knows little of that" - John Sturat Mill, English philosopher.

96

Further publications in 2011 and 2012

- → Managing Reward
- → Handling Discipline - *Best Practice*
- → Managing Diversity
- → Negotiating Skills
- → Burnout
- → Coaching Skills
- → Life Balance
- → Conflict Resolution
- → Influencing Skills
- → Mediation Skills
- → Assertiveness and Self-Esteem
- → Strategic Issue Communications
- → Personal Development
- → Innovation
- → Compliance
- → Strategy Development and Implementation
- → Leadership and Strategic Change
- → Managing with Impact - *Focusing on Performance through People*
- → Strategic Marketing
- → Entrepreneurial Skills
- → Managing Attendance at Work
- → Employee Relations
- → Improving your Writing Skills

- → Organisation Development/ Training
- → Change Management
- → Organisation Design
- → Energy Management
- → International Marketing
- → Governance in Today's Corporate World
- → Customer Relationship Management
- → Building Commitment to Quality
- → Understanding Finance
- → PR Skills for Managers
- → Logistics and Supply Chain
- → Dealing with Difficult People
- → Effective Meetings
- → Communication Skills
- → Facilitation Skills
- → Managing Upwards
- → Giving and Receiving Feedback
- → Consumer Behaviour
- → Delegation and Empowerment
- → Basic Economics for Managers
- → Finance for non Financial Executives
- → Business Forecasting
- → The Marketing of Services

Management Briefs
Essential Insights for Busy Managers

Our list of books already published includes:

- → Be Interview-Wise: *How to Prepare for and Manage Your Interviews*
  Brian McIvor

- → HR for Line Managers: *Best Practice*
  Frank Scott-Lennon & Conor Hannaway

- → Bullying & Harassment: *Values and Best Practice Responses*
  Frank Scott-Lennon & Margaret Considine

- → Career Detection: *Finding and Managing Your Career*
  Brian McIvor

- → Impactful Presentations: *Best Practice Skills*
  Yvonne Farrell

- → Project Management: *A Practical Guide*
  Dermot Duff & John Quilliam

- → Marketing Skills: *A Practical Guide*
  Garry Hynes & Ronan Morris

- → Performance Management: *Developing People and Performance*
  Frank Scott-Lennon & Fergus Barry

- → Proven Selling Skills: *For Winners*
  Ronan McNamara

- → Redundancy: *A Development Opportunity for You!*
  Frank Scott-Lennon, Fergus Barry & Brian McIvor

- → Safety Matters!: *A Guide to Health & Safety at Work*
  Adrian Flynn & John Shaw of Phoenix Safety

- → Time Matters: *Making the Most of Your Day*
  Julia Rowan

- → Emotional Intelligence (EQ): *A Leadership Imperative!*
  Daire Coffey & Deirdre Murray